ORGANISE
WITH JEN

ZONE CLEANING

THE ULTIMATE GUIDE

Your secret to maintaining a clean and tidy
home without the overwhelm.

JENNIFER NEAL

ORGANISE

WITH JEN

Dedicated to my wonderful zone cleaning community.
This book is for you.
Thank you for the suggestion and for giving me the confidence to write
a book. I hope it brings value to your life and serves as a token of my
appreciation for your incredible support.

With love and gratitude,
Jen

TESTIMONIALS

"I can be easily overwhelmed whilst cleaning. This reduces my stress and makes it enjoyable to complete!'
-Emma-

"What can I say...Jen is amazing! She makes decluttering and organising so achievable. Her approach of breaking down tasks into small chunks really helps to get the job done. Her friendly and warm personality make you feel like she's with you every step of the way. Life is definitely better when it's been organised with Jen!"
-Julie G-

"Jen's zone cleaning programme is full of short, manageable tasks. Say goodbye to cleaning overwhelm!"
-Karen-

"You inspired me just to clear my bedside table. You made me realise that I could do one job and stop without it being a massive job. This resulted in me decluttering my bedroom, living room and kitchen. You made it feel more manageable to start a task and then eventually maintain it. Thank you!"
-Siobhan-

"I love having Jen's zone cleaning schedules to help keep me on track. She is both practical and realistic with the goals she sets. The bite size chunks for cleaning and organising are easily achievable even with little time in the day to spare. Her zone cleaning has cured the overwhelm I used to feel when tackling cleaning and organising my home."
-Polly-

"Following Jen's zone cleaning has made me fall in love with my house again. I find the task lists easy to follow and not overwhelming for my busy life. Give it a try - you won't regret it. Thanks Jen x"
-Julie W-

CONTENTS

ZONE CLEANING

THE ULTIMATE GUIDE

Welcome!

Thank you for choosing this book and for joining me as we delve into the life-changing world of Zone Cleaning.

I'm Jen, a professional home organiser and founder of Organise With Jen, based in the west of Scotland. I provide a bespoke in-home and virtual decluttering and organising service, dedicated to enhancing your life at home. If you dream of having a calmer, tidier, more organised home that supports the life you want to live, I'm here to help you make it happen!

I've always been obsessed with organisation and optimising systems and routines to make looking after the home as easy as possible. Whilst being naturally tidy and organised, I also know how it feels to have spaces that are cluttered and out of control. It's not a great feeling! The good news is, after years of research, practice and fine-tuning, I learned how to change the habits that cause it and implement new strategies for maintaining a clean and clutter-free home with ease.

It led me to creating my very own simplified zone cleaning programme which revolutionised the way I approached decluttering, deep cleaning and tidying my home forever. Overwhelm, frustration and exhaustion became a thing of the past and now I actually feel excited to tackle the zone of the week! My hope, through the pages of this book, is that it will do the same for you.

During lockdown in 2020 and while spending so much time at home, I decided to share my seasonal zone cleaning programme on Instagram and Facebook in the hope that it would motivate and help people looking for an easier way. It wasn't long before a little community of enthusiastic, like-minded people started to follow along and join in with it. The feedback was positive and soon I was being asked if I could please put it all in a book!

Me? Write a book? Maybe one day...

And here it is! I can't quite believe it.

To Kenny and the boys, my family and friends and everyone who has supported me on this journey, thank you for believing in me and encouraging me to follow my dreams. Now I have a manual to give the boys when they eventually fly the nest! (I'm sure they'll be delighted!)

Lastly, I am incredibly grateful to YOU for being here. Your support means the world to me. I hope this book inspires you to try Zone Cleaning for yourself and witness the power it has to simplify your life, calm your space and clear your mind.

Are you ready to begin?

If you are looking for more tips and advice on how to organise your life, take a look at my website and blog:

http://organisewithjen.com

My intention for this book was for it to be an informative guide and companion to accompany my Zone Cleaning programme. It aims to inspire you to try Zone Cleaning and teach you strategies for simplifying your household chores and reducing overwhelm. It is full of practical tips and ideas to rewrite the rules and make cleaning and tidying as **easy** as possible. No more feeling guilty when you can't get everything done! The 'little and often' approach is the underlying theme of the book and is key to maintaining your home with ease. The more you clean, the less you'll clean and the easier it will be.

There is no finish line. Let's make decluttering and cleaning fun. Play your favourite music, sing, dance and enjoy the process.

The chapters that follow give you an insight into what zone cleaning is and how it works, the importance of daily and weekly routines and how to create a personalised cleaning schedule that's right for you. The Zone Cleaning Programme is presented in a step-by-step list format, ready for you to refer to as you put the plan into practice.

Life has a habit of being unpredictable, so I've also included a handy Home Reset guide for the times when your home has been a little neglected and feels out of control. This can be done at any time of year to whip your home into shape.

At the back of the book you will find ready-made checklists to track your progress and blank templates to customise your own zone clean and routines. There is also a section for you to make notes, journal, set goals and get intentional about your home. Have fun with it and don't forget to use a pencil so you can reuse the pages over and over.

Why not enjoy a bit of mindfulness colouring to personalise your book and bring the pages to life? There are lots of little sketch illustrations dotted throughout that you could be creative with if you feel like it.

Finally, you'll find an A-Z directory full of ideas for what to do with your decluttered items, to dispose of them responsibly and keep them out of landfill. I hope you find it useful.

Ultimately, I want this book to help you. I would love for you to have an open mind, take what you need from it and adapt it to create your own optimised cleaning schedule. A schedule that doesn't have you cleaning all day and leaves plenty of time for the things that really matter...like living your life and spending time with your loved ones.

My hope for you is that by consistently implementing the strategies from the zone cleaning programme, you will feel more relaxed about cleaning and more in control of your home generally. Bit by bit, you will gradually transform your living space into a more organised, serene and peaceful home you can live your best life in.

Happy reading!

Picture the scene. It's spring, the weather is bright and sunny and suddenly you feel the urge to open all the windows and clean the house from top to bottom. You buy tonnes of new cleaning products (you didn't really need), make a rough plan to get started, 'gie it laldy' for a few days, burn out, lose motivation and give up completely.

Yes, that was me! Can you relate?

Running a home and keeping on top of it all can feel like the hardest job in the world sometimes. I needed to find a way to get things done without running myself into the ground. I wanted to spend time with my children and husband, not clean all day long. You see, cleaning isn't something I *love* doing, but I do love a clean house! It took me years to understand that to have a clean house **and** maintain it with ease, it required me to be more organised and intentional about it.

I think it's important for your own sanity to let go of the idea that the whole house needs to be cleaned from top to bottom, all in one go, for it to be considered clean. For most of us, that's impossible to maintain anyway.

The bottom line is that cleaning will always need done. It's never going to be *'finished'*, so rather than burning yourself out trying to do it all at once or feeling that you need to clean the entire house on a weekly basis, think of it more as a rolling programme.

Several years ago, whilst researching the topics of cleaning routines and clutter-free living, I stumbled across a video on YouTube about Zone Cleaning. My eyes widened. *Zone Cleaning? What in the world was zone cleaning?* I had no idea, but I was intrigued and I needed to find out!

Zone Cleaning is an organised method for tidying and deep cleaning the home in simple, manageable steps.
The home is divided into zones and only one zone is tackled each week.

My Zone Cleaning routine is a cycle that is repeated 4 times throughout the year as a rolling programme, along with the changing seasons.
Each Zone Clean lasts 12 weeks.

Spring Zone Clean: March-May
Summer Zone Clean: June-Aug
Autumn Zone Clean: Sep-Nov
Winter Zone Clean: Dec-Feb or *Home Reset: Jan-Feb

What does zone cleaning look like on a day to day basis?
Your task each day is to declutter, tidy or clean in the zone for only 15-30 minutes, Mon-Fri, in **addition** to your usual daily/weekly cleaning. And that's it! If you work long hours during the week, simply set an hour or so aside at the weekend and do it then instead. It's completely flexible.

The lists for each zone contain *'suggested tasks'* of things that would normally need attention every 3-6 months, typically the types of jobs you would do monthly, seasonally or while spring cleaning e.g. cleaning windows, wiping down skirting boards and editing your wardrobe.

The zone clean is NOT a daily or weekly cleaning routine. It does not cover the things that need done every single day or week, like laundry, washing dishes or ironing.

At first, Zone Cleaning will feel like a boot camp for your house but eventually, if you stick with it and make it a habit, you will naturally slip into maintenance mode. Maintenance mode is when your home has reached a baseline of clean, tidy and well maintained 'most' of the time. Remember we're not aiming for perfection here, it doesn't exist. Your home is for living in! It's going to get messy and dirty.

Little and often' is my mantra for all household chores. When things are attended to on a regular basis, everything is easier and more manageable. Over time, you will become so familiar with the zones and routines that you will just instinctively know what needs to be done on any given day or week. You'll find you won't need to rely on the checklists quite as much and habits that felt difficult in the beginning, will become automatic.

Starting is the hardest part and zone cleaning helps with that. It is motivating because the tasks are short and achievable and it frees your mind to focus on one area and one task at a time. You do one task and stop. That's right! You do *not* need to go on and clean the entire room on the same day. It is so liberating!

The beauty of the rolling programme is that it doesn't matter if you don't get everything done on the list on any given week. Do what you can and pick up where you left off next season, when it starts all over again.

There's no such thing as telling yourself, 'I just can't do it' or 'I don't have time to do it', because with zone cleaning, there's no pressure to do it **all**.

"Time is a created thing. To say 'I don't have time,' is like saying, 'I don't want to."- Lao Tzu

Be mindful of the stories you tell yourself!

The thing is, doing something is better than doing nothing and what I know for sure is that with the Zone Cleaning method, I achieve a lot more than I would if I wasn't following it, if that makes sense!

Of course there will be times when you actually won't have time, and that's okay too, that's life. We'll cover that further on in the book. For me, Zone Cleaning was the answer I'd been searching for all along! Keep reading to find out why I had to make it my own...

Have you ever tried a cleaning routine that didn't work? Me too! Cleaning routines are available everywhere. If you want one, you don't need to look far. Google it and you'll be inundated with cleaning routines on YouTube, Instagram, Facebook, Amazon, blogs, apps...many offering free printables and checklists to go with them. Fantastic, right? They *are* great, yes. I've probably tried most of them. I even bought an app that I *really* thought would be amazing...

BUT

...even though it's a really great app, well designed and well thought out etc, it's not amazing for *me*. The plan just doesn't suit my lifestyle and home set up. I've started and restarted it many times - usually on a Monday, determined to make it work - but by Tuesday I feel like I've failed. And that's the first problem with cleaning routines - we feel like a failure and give up when they don't work! Sounds dramatic, but it's true.

The interesting thing is, I have NEVER found a cleaning routine designed by someone else that worked perfectly for me and offered me long term success. They are all motivating, at first, until something else gets in the way (like my busy life) and BOOM! It's already not working and I've lost motivation.

If this is something you've found to be true for you as well, I hear you, you're definitely not alone.

The trouble with cleaning routines is not in the routines themselves but rather the fact that WE are all UNIQUE. We think differently, live different lives, have different jobs, different homes, different lifestyles and different responsibilities.

A routine that suits one, will not suit another.

With all that said, do I think my Zone Cleaning Programme will work perfectly as it is, for every single person who reads this book and tries it?

No, absolutely not! It won't be for everyone.

But what I do know is that there will be something in this book that will help you. The principles behind zone cleaning are truly life-changing and it is very easy to adapt. There's no one size fits all when it comes to cleaning and organising. You have to find what works for you.

This means, if you want a cleaning routine to work, it needs to suit your preferences and unique set of circumstances. This is exactly what I had to do when I started experimenting with zone cleaning.

'Zone Cleaning' is not a new idea and it's not my idea. As I mentioned before, there is a plethora of resources out there, all on the topic of cleaning and zone cleaning.

The problem with all the zone cleaning routines I tried, was that they seemed unnecessarily overcomplicated and many assumed I was at home all day, which I wasn't. I needed a simpler formula. A formula that worked with my busy life. I set about creating my own routine that was simple, easy to follow and covered all the main areas of the home, one at a time.

The zone cleaning routine I share with you now in this book is based on the original I created for myself back then but it has been adapted slightly over time. Why? Trial and error. Following the routine highlighted what worked well and what needed to change. The routine has been optimised, tweaked, edited and improved into the Ultimate Seasonal Zone Cleaning Programme you see before you today. I'm confident that it is simple to follow and will help make decluttering and cleaning more manageable and enjoyable for you.

The programme has only become what it is today because of the constructive and helpful feedback I have received from the many women in my online community who have tried the programme and loved it.

We had a common goal in mind to make it the best zone cleaning routine it could be and now it is here, designed to be adapted by YOU, so you can make it your own!

I really hope you love it too.

There's more to keeping on top of a home than zone cleaning alone. Zone Cleaning is what I call the third layer of the system - and the icing on the cake. There are specific household tasks we need to do every single day to look after a home - first layer. These are the core habits that keep your home functioning well, day to day. Then there are the jobs we need to take care of weekly or fortnightly - second layer. These are the tidying and cleaning jobs that take care of the surfaces and floors in the different rooms in your house. Once you have good habits and routines established in layers one and two, implementing the third layer, the zone clean, is easy and takes care of everything else that needs done on an occasional basis.

Let's talk about how to fit zone cleaning around your existing routines. And if you're thinking, 'Help!' I don't have any routines, don't worry, we'll cover how to get started with that in the next chapter.

Zone cleaning means dividing your home up into rooms or areas and focusing on only one zone each week, in addition to your normal daily/weekly cleaning. The beauty of it is that you only spend a short amount of time tackling something from the zone each day, so it is fairly easy to fit it in, even if you work outside the home.

Chipping away at these third layer tasks, is the secret to maintaining your home with ease. When you leave things for too long and let clutter and dirt build up, there's much more effort and time required to deal with it effectively. It becomes a huge, burdensome task you don't want to do.

When it comes to your daily tasks, you probably already have specific things you do every day on repeat without having to think about it too much. These habits form the first layer of your daily routine. Within these daily habits it can be helpful to establish a basic morning and evening routine to help you plan and prepare effectively for the day ahead.

"Either you run the day or the day runs you." - Jim Rohn

Tomorrow starts today. Firstly, there are things you can do the night before to ensure a smooth start to the next morning e.g. empty the dishwasher, prepare lunches, check your planner to see what you have scheduled for the next day, take tomorrow's dinner out the freezer, check the weather forecast and look out what you're going to wear, set out your keys and bag and set the breakfast table.

Likewise there are things you can do in the morning that will make you feel more productive and in control of your day, such as making your bed, checking your schedule, planning and prepping dinner, popping a load of laundry on etc.

Once you have embedded these helpful practices into your daily routine, they will become automatic and it will be easier to see where you have the space and time to carry out your weekly and zone cleaning tasks. Some of the daily tasks will only take a few minutes while the weekly tasks are likely to take a bit longer. If you want housework-free weekends, it means your weekly and zone cleaning tasks should be done Mon-Fri.

If you've never timed yourself to see how long it takes you to do certain tasks, I highly recommend it. It will help you plan more effectively. No point in a 5 minute slot to clean your toilets and sinks, if you have 3 bathrooms and it takes you 20 minutes in real time!

I've included some examples over the next few pages, of daily and weekly routines that you might find helpful.

For a good solid weekly routine, it's important to make a list of the rooms in your house you need to clean and work out which days suit you best. Will the room need cleaned every week? Or would fortnightly suffice? I have also included an alternative weekly cleaning routine which focusses on cleaning by task, rather than by room.

Remember there's no one size fits all with this. Just because your friend changes her bed sheets every week and cleans out her fridge on a Friday doesn't mean you have to. You do you and let her be her.

Be aware that some areas of your home will require less cleaning than others. This is dependent on how the space is used and how often. What I know for sure, is that minimal clutter on your surfaces will make cleaning infinitely easier.

As a general rule:
Do the **minimum** possible to keep your home at a baseline level of clean and tidy that's right for you. If something doesn't need cleaned, don't clean it - even if it's on a zone cleaning list!

Likewise, if you notice something needs cleaned, no matter which zone it is in, clean it as soon as you can to avoid it getting worse or making it more difficult than it needs to be.

You can do your zone cleaning at any time of day that suits you. Sometimes I like getting it done first thing in the morning, if I'm up early and feeling productive, and other times I am so busy during the week, I have to do it at the weekend instead. Some weeks I get it all done and some weeks I only manage one or two things from the list. It really doesn't matter.

If I am away on holiday for a week or a fortnight, those zones get missed out completely. And it's absolutely fine! It can't be avoided and it's no problem because it's a rolling programme. There's no such thing as 'catching up' with the zone cleaning programme. Remember there's no finish line. Each week is a clean slate. You move on and start fresh in the new zone, no matter what you did or didn't do the week before.

Be flexible and above all else, give yourself grace and be kind to yourself. If you need a rest, listen to your body and take it. There's no 'cleaning police'. Nobody is coming to check to see what you have or haven't done.

Some people believe that systems, routines and schedules are limiting and restrictive but the opposite is true. They help us streamline what we need to do and provide structure and organisation to our lives, whilst also allowing room for flexibility.

Systems and routines are time-saving and necessary if you want to be organised and keep your home clean and tidy. They can help you manage your tasks more efficiently, and when you do follow a schedule it takes the guesswork out of it. If you take the time to plan what you want to get done and consider the timeframe you have to do it, it allows you to break down the tasks into manageable chunks and spread them over different days or weeks.

This is how you can successfully reduce overwhelm and avoid stressful, frantic cleaning sessions when you are short of time or when visitors are coming over. It also ensures that everything gets done regularly and nothing is overlooked or neglected.

When you fail to plan, you plan to fail. With no routine, system or formula to follow, it means things either get done on an adhoc basis or they don't get done at all. You will also have more thoughts swirling around your mind, which can lead to feeling out of control with everything you have to do.

Having routines and systems in place contributes to your overall health and well-being. When you are on top of everything, you feel calmer, happier and more relaxed and you will cope better when life throws you a curve ball (which it will).

The zone cleaning routine and home reset in this book are provided for you to use as a guide and to change as you see fit. Adapt them to make them work for you, your home and your lifestyle.

HOW TO SET UP SYSTEMS AND ROUTINES THAT WORK FOR YOU

Here are some tips to help you create a cleaning routine that works for you:

It's all about flexibilty, adaptation and personalisation to suit your preferences, schedule and priorities. It will change over time as your circumstance change and you transition from one season of life to another.

Consider the 3 layers of the overall process...

- Daily Routine
- Weekly Routine
- Zone Cleaning Routine

1. Assess your home's needs and compile a list of tasks that need to be done daily, weekly, monthly/seasonally (the latter are your zone clean tasks).
2. Be realistic about the time you have available and factor in your other responsibilities, energy levels and when you are at your most motivated. No overwhelming yourself with a routine you won't be able to keep up with.
3. Create a schedule that outlines the tasks you plan to do and when you will do them.
4. Be kind to yourself. If you can't manage to fit in your weekly tasks, spread them out over a fortnight instead. Allow room for flexibility and remember that life can get in the way sometimes. It's okay if you miss something or need to adjust. Aim to get back on track as soon as you can and it really won't matter.
5. You don't need to do it all yourself. Enlist the help of family members or hire a cleaner for specific jobs, if you need to lighten the load. Never feel guilty about doing this, it's not a sign of weakness but a symbol of strength.
10. Review, edit and adjust your cleaning routine as necessary to address your changing needs and keep yourself motivated.

DAILY HABITS & ROUTINES for a clean and tidy home

This will be similar for everyone but some things may not need done as often or at all if your lifestyle or home set up does not require it.

Example:

- Make bed
- Load of laundry/ironing/folding and putting away
- Bathroom quick clean - toilet, sink & straighten things up
- Plan dinner
- Dishes, sink and kitchen surfaces
- Clean hob after cooking
- Vacuum/mop as necessary
- Deal with mail
- Tidy as you go
- Put toys away

WEEKLY HABITS & ROUTINES for a clean and tidy home

Again, this will be different for everyone depending on your home set-up and lifestyle. It can be done on a weekly or fortnightly basis. Generally speaking your weekly cleaning routine is concerned with the rooms you need to clean and will deal with the dust and grime on the surfaces and floor. Remember to always tidy before you clean and create a plan that works for you. There's no right or wrong way.

Example:

Mon - Kitchen
Tue- Living room/Dining Room
Wed - Bedroom(s) (Change sheets every 1-2 wks)
Thu - Bathroom(s) /Ironing
Fri - Hall & Entryway
Sat - No cleaning/ Water Houseplants
Sun - No cleaning

ALTERNATIVE EXAMPLE OF A WEEKLY CLEANING ROUTINE

Rather than focussing on one room per day for your weekly house cleaning, you could try this alternative method of cleaning by task instead. Start in one area of your home and always move around in the same order.

Example:

Mon - Dust
Tue- Mirrors, glass and screens
Wed - Bathrooms
Thu - Vacuum
Fri - Mop hard floors
Sat - Change Sheets
Sun - No Cleaning

EXAMPLE OF A BATHROOM CLEANING ROUTINE

Bathrooms generally need some attention every day, especially if you live in a busy house. If you have one bathroom, this is fairly manageable but if you have multiple bathrooms it is a lot more work and considerably more time-consuming.

How often you should clean your bathroom is not an exact science. There's no one rule or routine that will suit everyone. It's also going to be different for each household depending on how much use each bathroom gets. A whole family sharing one bathroom will need a lot more attention than a bathroom used by one person.

I have 3 bathrooms to look after in my house, so I will share how I break up the tasks over the course of the week Mon -Fri to make it easier to manage.

Every day, or at least every other day, I do a quick clean of the toilets and sinks. This is easy and each one only takes a few minutes as it's done regularly. In addition to this basic routine, I try to cover the rest of the weekly bathroom tasks by doing **one** other thing each day...

Mon - Mirrors
Tue - Tub
Wed - Windows
Thu - nothing extra today
Fri - Floors

On Mondays and Fridays I change the towels, wipe down the towel radiators and empty the bins. This method means I don't ever have to clean whole bathrooms at once or have a bathroom cleaning day.

Let's talk about a Simple Daily Routine.

We already know there's no such thing as being completely done when it comes to housework, but the ideas that follow should help you establish a simple baseline routine that works for you, your home and your family.

One of the best tips I can give you before you get started is to tidy nightly, especially if you are a busy mum. Give yourself a head start in the morning by preparing what you can the night before.

Pick up on your way to bed. It only takes a few minutes to straighten things up and put stray items where they belong. Lay out yours and your children's clothes, shoes, bags for the next day etc. This will make your mornings so much easier from the get go.

The daily routine outlined on the following page is the minimum required to maintain an orderly home and shouldn't take long. The jobs are the same every day and can be done at any time of day. When tackling each job, move fast, don't get distracted and use a timer if it helps.

It can be motivating and fun to use a timer at first just to see how long it actually takes to do each job.

EXAMPLE OF A SIMPLE DAILY ROUTINE

BEDROOMS
- Make bed
- Sort dirty clothes and do one load of laundry

BATHROOMS
- Quick clean of toilet & sink
- Clean mirror, if required
- Straighten towels or change them, if required

LIVING ROOM
- Straighten cushions, blankets and throws
- Tidy away anything that doesn't belong

KITCHEN
- Wash, dry and put away dishes after meals and fill and empty dishwasher as required
- Wipe down worktop and hob
- Change cloths and towels, if required

FLOORS
- Quick sweep/hoover of main areas, if required. Mop weekly if you have hard floors.

GENERAL
- Open and deal with mail immediately

IRONING
- Try to iron as you go. A little each day or most days is preferable to a massive overwhelming mountain by the end of the week. If the pile is large to begin with, set a 15 minute timer and do as many items as you can. Repeat as often as you can throughout the day to reduce the pile. Fold and put away laundered clothes.

HOW TO SET UP SYSTEMS AND ROUTINES THAT WORK FOR YOU

BUSY MUM LAUNDRY ROUTINE

Aim to do ONE load of laundry per day.
(Washing is a rolling programme - also known as never ending!)

When you have a lot of laundry to deal with, the goal is NOT to empty the laundry basket completely every day. That's impossible to maintain when you have a million other things to do.
Simply by doing a little each day you will maintain it at a level that feels manageable.

- Gather all the family's dirty laundry in one spot and sort into three piles, whites, colours and darks.
- Wash the largest pile and tip the rest back into the dirty laundry bin for the next day.
- Try to sort the wet washing as you hang it up to dry eg hang all the items that will require ironing together, towels together, all socks together, all underwear together, all sportswear together. This works whether you hang it outside or inside and makes it quicker and easier to deal with when dry.
- Once the washing is dry, set the garments aside that will require ironing.
- Sort and fold all other items into separate piles for each family member to put away.
- Iron clothing and linens and put away. Job done and no ironing pile that grows as the week goes on!

In an effort to reduce the amount of laundry you have to deal with, think about how often you and your family are wearing or using items before washing. Not everything will need washed after one wear. Children can be especially guilty of wearing something once and throwing it in the laundry bin or floor. They don't care about laundry or think like adults, but the good news is, they can be trained!

If you work outside the home during the day and don't start the laundry until you come home in the evening, you will probably need to set time aside the next day to sort, fold, iron, and put away.

If you feel you've got the laundry under control after trying this method for a few weeks, you might find you can have a laundry free day at the weekend. This won't mean your laundry bin is empty, just that you are on top of everything enough to leave it for a day. How good would that be?

Remember this is just a guide. There are no *rules*. You don't need to change everything you are doing all at once. Start small, and try one new thing. See how it goes and then try adding something else into the routine. By trying to implement a routine like this, you will feel less overwhelmed and more in control of your day, your home and your life. If you don't have much time to do everything at once, break it up into small manageable chunks throughout the day or over the course of the week.

Starting is the hardest part but restarting is even harder. If some days you don't have time to do it all, that's fine, let it go and don't worry about it. Just try your best to get back on track the next day.

The more you get used to a routine, the easier and quicker it is to stick to it.

I'm not here to tell you which cleaning products you should or shouldn't use, but what I will say is...

Keep. It. Simple.

Cleaning is a chore that most of us would happily avoid if we could and what makes cleaning feel even worse is when your cleaning supplies are overcrowded, cluttered and disorganised. We're led to believe we need lots of different fancy, colourful cleaning products in order to keep a clean house, when it's simply not true. Most of us could drastically reduce the number of products we use by simplifying our kit and routine. I can't tell you the last time I used a window cleaning product or a stainless steel cleaner for example, they're just not necessary anymore. Microfibre cloths do the job just as well, if not even better! Also, one of the most basic cleaners we all have in our homes, dishwashing liquid, can be used as an all-purpose cleaner all around the home. Yes, there are some task-specific cleaners you may need for some jobs, but on the whole, the simplest products are the best. If you like the idea of cleaning naturally, then baking soda, white vinegar, lemons and essential oils are going to be your best friends! You could even experiment and make your own simple counter top spray for very little cost. I sometimes make my own but if I am looking to buy, I try to go for products that are eco-friendly and refillable. Something simple, natural and multi-purpose that can do the job of many is a godsend and frees up so much space in the cleaning cupboard too!

CONSIDER MICROFIBRE & CHEMICAL FREE CLEANING

Another way to create space in your cleaning cupboard is by ditching traditional cleaners and switching to microfibre cloths. I LOVE a microfibre cloth! They clean effectively with water alone and remove 99% of germs and bacteria without chemicals. Backed by science, it's a purse-friendly option that's healthier for your family, more sustainable and kinder to the planet. Microfibre cloths are reusable and can simply be washed in the machine after use. Imagine, no more wipes or plastic bottles and no more nasty chemicals being sprayed in your home, polluting the air you breathe.

THE SEASONAL
ZONE CLEANING PROGRAMME

My Seasonal Zone Cleaning Programme is a simple plan that is repeated 4 times throughout the year.

It runs with the seasons and each one lasts 12 weeks.

Where and when to begin.
You can start the zone cleaning programme at any time of year but it is easiest if you start at the beginning of a new season.
Begin Week 1, Zone 1 on the first Monday of any new season and follow on from there. For example, if the first Monday in March is the 3rd, that's when you will begin the spring zone clean, and so on. You will find if you follow it all the way through to zone 12, there will be a week or two at the end where there will be no zone cleaning to be done before the next season begins. Enjoy a complete break and allow yourself to rest and recharge during these weeks, you deserve it!

Spring Zone Clean: March-May
Summer Zone Clean: June-Aug
Autumn Zone Clean: Sep-Nov
Winter Zone Clean: Dec-Feb or *Home Reset: Jan-Feb

*If like me, you like the idea of a complete break in December, you can do the shorter 8 week Home Reset Plan in Jan/Feb instead of the full 12 week Winter Zone Clean. Whatever works best for you. Don't worry, you'll find the all the details of the Home Reset further on in the book. It's a simpler, shorter version of the zone clean and can be done at any time of year if your home needs it.

If there's one thing I want you to take away from this book, it's that zone cleaning is about making cleaning, decluttering and tidying easier and in a way that feels manageable. Try the templates and checklists, tweak to suit and make it your own.

Okay, are you ready to take a look at the zones and get started...

THE ZONES

Zone 1: Kitchen

Zone 2: Kitchen (part 2)

Zone 3: Living Room

Zone 4: Dining Room and/or Home Office

Zone 5: Seasonal Wardrobe Edit

Zone 6: Main Bedroom

Zone 7: Kid's Room or Guest Room

Zone 8: Bathroom

Zone 9: Hall, Stairs & Entryway

Zone 10: Utility/Laundry Room

Zone 11: Paperwork or Own Choice (play room, hobby room etc)

Zone 12: Car/Garage/Shed/Outside Space

THE SEASONAL
ZONE CLEANING PROGRAMME

THE PROCESS

You will notice at the top of each zone's list, the first two suggested tasks are concerned with **decluttering**. A surface declutter followed by a cupboard or drawer declutter.

There is a reason for this...

DECLUTTERING - ORGANISING - TIDYING - CLEANING

The 4 processes above are each an important component of looking after and maintaining a home, but they are all different.

Often these four steps are lumped together as one, and thought of simply as 'cleaning'. This makes the job more difficult than it needs to be and limits the progress possible. When you do it like this you'll find yourself going round in circles, getting distracted and struggling to feel any sense of lasting achievement. The order we do things in really does make a difference to the outcome. If you try to clean a cluttered, messy room, you'll get nowhere fast! Decluttering regularly is fundamental to making everything else easier.

DECLUTTERING deals with the removal and letting go of unnecessary items

ORGANISING deals with giving everything a home

TIDYING deals with neatening and putting objects away

CLEANING deals with dirt

To be able to CLEAN quickly and effectively, it has to be the LAST step in the process.

THE SEASONAL ZONE CLEANING PROGRAMME

THE PROCESS

Now when you tackle your zone cleaning or any other sort of cleaning, I suggest you do the decluttering and tidying first and then you'll be able to clean everything else on the list more easily and without distraction.

I usually try to do the surface declutter on a Monday and the cabinet or drawer declutter on the Tuesday. After that I pick and choose from the list as I please.

Each day...

Pick from the list
Allow 15-30 minutes
Set a timer
Move fast
Stay focussed and don't get distracted
Try to avoid skipping ahead and doing too much in one day.

Short and manageable is what you're looking for, that's what will keep you motivated and give you time for your other daily and weekly routines and living your life!

If you come to a zone in your home that is out of control and feels too cluttered to clean, forget cleaning and simply focus on decluttering in there each day instead. It's impossible to clean a messy home quickly, easily or effectively. Decluttering is the first step you should to take.

Use the ready made checklists at the back of the book to keep track of your progress or customise your own using the blank templates.

THE ZONES

ZONE 1
The Kitchen

Surface Declutter

Cabinet/drawer declutter

Ceiling/walls/lighting

Windows/window treatments

Doors & woodwork

Cabinet & drawer fronts

Counter tops & splash back

Seasonal Zone Clean
Week 1 Kitchen:

Welcome to Week 1, Zone 1

We start with the kitchen and because it's the most complex, we stay in there for 2 weeks. This week's list covers the kitchen itself and next week's list covers the appliances and other elements within the kitchen.

Surface Declutter
It's always a good idea to start in a new zone with a surface declutter. When you come to clean it, it will be easier if you do this first.

Look at your kitchen with a fresh pair of eyes.

Where are the problem areas?
Does it look too busy?
Is there anything you no longer use taking up valuable worktop space that you could get rid of?
Has anything migrated there from other rooms in the house?
How does it make you feel?
Think about how you want it to look and feel.

Remove surface clutter from the counter tops, above wall cabinets, on the shelves and from the floor.

Bag up anything for donation.
Relocate items to their proper home.
Recycle what you can.
Bin anything that can't be saved.

Cabinet / Drawer Declutter

Is there a cupboard or drawer in your kitchen that's driving you mad? Do the contents belong there or is a reshuffle required? Let's get it sorted!

Empty it, sort through the contents and declutter. Categorise and organise the items you love, use and need and return them to the space if it makes sense for them to be there.

Use small boxes, lids, or containers to create organised compartments inside drawers and why not try a lazy susan or two inside cupboards to keep the space tidy.

Bag up anything for donation.
Relocate items to their proper home.
Recycle what you can.
Bin anything that can't be saved.

Ceiling, Walls & Lighting

This should only need done once or twice a year, so keep a note on your checklist when you do it. Dust the ceilings and walls using a long handled fluffy duster, a pillowcase or microfibre cloth on the end of a broom or your vacuum cleaner tools.

Work in a clockwise direction, starting at the top and working your way down, going right into the corners. Get rid of the cobwebs and be careful around your lights.

For the lighting, a damp microfibre cloth should do the trick. Microfibre cloths designed for cleaning glass are perfect for glass shades. A lint roller is a fantastic tool for removing dust from fabric shades.

Seasonal Zone Clean
Week 1 Kitchen:

Windows and Window Treatments

Kitchen windows get grimy and dirty very easily, especially if they are near the sink or hob, so it's a good idea to try to do them every time the zone comes round. Cleaning the inside of your windows and giving your blinds a quick wipe, dust or vacuum every season will help you keep on top of it and prevent the dirt from building up too much.

Use your favourite glass cleaner or simply wash the glass with warm water (with a tiny dash of dishwashing detergent in it) and a microfibre cloth. Don't forget the frames, handles and ledges too! A microfibre cloth designed for glass, will dry and polish the windows off and make them sparkle.

A lint roller will work well for removing dust from fabric blinds.

Doors and Woodwork

Doors and woodwork can be cleaned with warm soapy water and a clean cloth. A microfibre cloth will trap the dirt easily and leave the surface streak free. Don't forget the door frames, tops and edges and handles.

Scuff marks can be hard to remove from painted doors so you may need to try a stronger product like a cream cleaner or cleaning paste. Always check on an inconspicuous area first as they can be abrasive.

If your skirting boards are dusty, vacuum first with the soft brush attachment, then wipe down with a damp cloth.

Cabinets and Drawer Fronts

Drawer fronts and cabinet doors can be cleaned quickly with warm soapy water and a clean cloth. A microfibre cloth will trap the dirt easily and leave the surface streak free. Don't forget the tops, edges and handles.

A word on open shelving:

Shelves take a lot of work to maintain, especially in a kitchen. Everything on them gathers dust and unless they are kept tidy, they can make a room feel cluttered and busy and add a significant amount of time onto your cleaning routine. Just something to keep in mind if you are planning a new kitchen or redesigning your space.

Clear your shelves, dusting/wiping items as you go.
Wipe the shelves down and return only the items you love, use and need. Less is more.

Counter Tops and Splash Back

Clear and clean your counter tops and splash back one section at a time. Warm soapy water and a dishcloth will do nicely or use a microfibre cloth to trap the dirt easily and leave the surface streak free.

Move anything sitting out on your surfaces as you go, wipe down small appliances and empty the crumbs from your toaster.

ZONE 2
The Kitchen
(Part 2)

Pantry Declutter

Microwave

Oven & Hob

Fridge/Freezer

Dishwasher

Sink Unit

Bin

Floor

Seasonal Zone Clean
Week 2: Kitchen

Pantry

The pantry or food cupboard can seem like a big job, but even just tidying and cleaning one section of it will be worth it. You don't have to tackle the whole thing in one go. Look and see where the need is.

Take everything out and set aside, decluttering as you go. Get rid of expired food, duplicates of kitchen gadgets and anything you no longer use, love or need.

Clean the shelves and cupboard interior. Categorise what you are keeping before reorganising everything back inside. Store like with like and use containers and turntables where appropriate to keep categories separate and everything organised.
Label the containers. This may seem unnecessary but it's a game changer, I promise.

Microwave

Tips for easy microwave maintenance...

Best time to clean your microwave is when it has just been used and is warm inside. Get into the habit of wiping it down after use or when you're clearing up after a meal. Always use microwaveable plate covers when cooking to avoid splatters.

If it's in a bad state, pop some sliced citrus fruit in a microwaveable bowl with a little water in it. Microwave uncovered for 2 minutes and leave to sit with the door shut for another few minutes to help soften burnt on splashes and food particles. Use a non-scratch scrubber and warm soapy water to clean the microwave before rinsing and drying off with a microfibre cloth.

Oven & Hob

Tips for cleaning your oven

Start by removing the metal racks, shelves and grill pan. Put in the dishwasher if they fit and while it's on, get to work cleaning the oven interior.

An excellent natural cleaner for your oven is baking soda and clear, white vinegar. Sprinkle a fine layer of baking soda onto the base of the oven and glass door. Spray with white vinegar until you hear it start to fizz and bubble. Leave it to work its magic for 15 minutes, then scrub with a non-scratch scrubber to easily remove burnt on residues. Scrub the rest of the oven interior with the same scrubber before rinsing everything away with warm water and a damp microfibre cloth. A lovely, natural and effective way to get the job done.

When you bring the grill pan and oven racks out the dishwasher you will notice they will probably still need some work to remove burnt on residue. Popping in the dishwasher first reduces the amount of elbow grease required to clean them afterwards. For stubborn residue on trays and grill pans, try soaking in warm water with a dishwasher tablet for a few hours before scrubbing and rinsing or pop back into the dishwasher.

Cleaning pastes are my favourite type of product for cleaning metal oven racks and the metal gas burner rings on the hob.
Just remember not to use anything abrasive on surfaces with a glossy finish. Racks from gas hobs are usually dishwasher safe and your extractor fan may have removable filters that can also be put in the dishwasher for a thorough cleaning. Check the manufacturer's instructions. Cooker hoods get grimy very quickly so it's best to keep them looking good by simply wiping over with a microfibre cloth rinsed in warm soapy water, weekly or fortnightly.

Seasonal Zone Clean
Week 2: Kitchen

Fridge / Freezer

If this is the first time you've tried the Zone Clean, you may feel you want to do both the fridge and the freezer but it'll take longer than 15-30 minutes if you do. Be kind to yourself. Do what you can and leave the rest for the next time. I make it as easy as possible for myself and rarely do both. I usually choose to do one or the other.

Fridge Tips

It can be overwhelming if you bring all the food out at the same time so do one section at a time to make it easier. And don't forget to keep it cool by avoiding the fridge door lying open for too long.

Remove the contents and check expiry dates. Discard anything you won't eat or won't use anymore.

Categorise items you are putting back in and think about investing in fridge storage to keep it organised going forward.

The right storage products should make life easier, so think carefully about what you need before purchasing and always measure first!

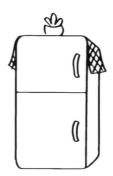

How to store your food safely in the fridge...

Fridge Storage Tips
The FSA (Food Standards Agency) recommends the ideal temp for your fridge is between 3-5 deg celsius

UPPER SHELVES
Foods that don't require cooking such as cooked meats and left-overs

MIDDLE / LOWER SHELVES
Dairy - milk, cheese, butter, yoghurt

BOTTOM SHELF
(coldest)
Raw meat, poultry, fish, wrapped or in sealed containers.

DRAWERS
Veg, salad, herbs, fruit

DOOR SHELVES
(warmest)
Foods that have natural preservatives, condiments, jams, juice

It is NOT recommended to keep avocados, bananas, nectarines, peaches, pears, plums and tomatoes in the fridge. This is due to the gas they release which can make other fruits and veggies spoil prematurely.

Current guidelines state that milk should not be stored in the fridge door as it can be susceptible to temperature fluctuations. Sometimes however it's unavoidable if your fridge has no other space tall enough for milk bottles.

According to nhs.uk, eggs are best stored in the fridge to keep them fresher and at a constant temperature. Bring them to room temperature before cooking.

Seasonal Zone Clean
Week 2: Kitchen

Dishwasher

Wipe down the exterior and door edges regularly to prevent a build up of food splashes and grime.

Once a month, remove the filter and clear away any food debris before cleaning with a soft toothbrush and warm soapy water.

Run a maintenance wash to clean your dishwasher naturally with vinegar and baking soda...

Do this when your dishwasher is empty.

Place a dishwasher safe bowl with clear white vinegar on the top rack and run a long, hot cycle.

For extra freshness, follow this by sprinkling a cup of baking soda on the bottom of the empty dishwasher and run a short, quick cycle.

Sink Unit

Remove everything from the sink area, cleaning items as you go. Wipe down the surfaces around the sink thoroughly.

Empty the under sink cupboard and declutter.

Wash the interior and leave to dry while you sort out and categorise the items you want to keep. Before you put everything back, give the sink and splash back a good scrub paying particular attention to the taps and plug hole.

To clean and freshen the drain, pop a cup of soda crystals or baking soda down the plughole and leave for 20 minutes, then flush away with hot water from the kettle.

Reorganise your under sink cupboard with only the items you need and use regularly.

Bin

Empty the bin and take the rubbish out.
Wash the interior, exterior and lid of the bin with warm soapy water and a microfibre cloth.

Dry thoroughly before popping a fresh bin bag inside.

If your bin has spills or stains inside it you may need something a bit stronger to clean it and a disinfectant to remove germs.

Floor

Vacuum the floor thoroughly to pick up crumbs, dust and cobwebs and use the crevice tool to get right under the furniture, into the corners and along the edges.

Mop or wash hard floors.

Mops can often miss the edges and corners of a room. It's a good idea during a zone clean to get a floor cloth and go down on your hands and knees to remove any residual dirt or crumbs from these awkward spots.

ZONE 3
The Living Room

Surface declutter

Cabinet/drawer declutter

Ceiling, Walls & Lighting

Windows/window treatments

Upholstery/soft furnishings

Doors & Woodwork

Fireplace

Floor

Seasonal Zone Clean
Week 3: Living Room

Surface Declutter

Let's start with a surface declutter of your living room.
Stand at the door and look at it with a fresh pair of eyes as though you were a visitor.

Where are the problem areas?
Does it look too busy?
How does it make you feel?
Think about how you want it to look and feel.

Is there anything you no longer use taking up valuable space that you could get rid of?

Are there too many things sitting out gathering dust? Decor pieces you've grown tired of?

How about excess furniture or placement of furniture?

Could you remove anything or rearrange to make better use of space?

Remove surface clutter from tables, cabinets, shelves and floor.

This is a simply a clearing and tidying job, not a cleaning job.

Bag up anything for donation.
Relocate items to their proper home.
Recycle what you can.
Bin anything that can't be saved.

Cabinet or Drawer Declutter

Is there a cabinet, drawer or shelf in your living room driving you mad? It's time to deal with it today. Empty it. Sort through the contents and declutter. Categorise and organise the items you love, use and need and return them to the space if they belong. Use drawer organisers or small boxes and lids to create compartments within drawers and on shelves. This will help to keep the space tidy and organised.

Bag up anything for donation.
Relocate items to their proper home.
Recycle what you can.
Bin anything that can't be saved.

Ceiling, Walls & Lighting

This only needs done once or twice a year, so make a note on your checklist when you do it, so you can remember.

Dust ceilings and walls using a long handled fluffy duster, a microfibre cloth or pillowcase on the end of a broom or your vacuum cleaner tools. Move around the room in a clockwise direction, starting at the top and working your way down, getting right into the corners. Get rid of cobwebs and be careful around lights.

For the lighting, warm soapy water and a damp, well wrung out microfibre cloth should be enough. If your shades can be removed for cleaning, do it because it will be easier than standing with your hands above your head.

Microfibre cloths designed for cleaning glass are good for leaving glass fixtures and glass shades streak free.

A lint roller is the perfect tool for removing dust from fabric lamp shades.

Seasonal Zone Clean
Week 3: Living Room

Windows and Window Treatments

Keep your windows looking nice with a clean every season. It will make them easier to clean and help prevent the dirt from building up too much.

For the windows, use your favourite window cleaner or simply wash with warm water (with a tiny dash of dishwashing detergent in it) and a microfibre cloth. Wash the glass panes first with the damp cloth and then use a glass cleaning cloth to dry and polish them off and make them sparkle! Wipe down the window frames, handles and ledges thoroughly.

A lint roller is fantastic for removing dust from fabric blinds and curtains. The soft brush attachment on your vacuum cleaner will do a good job too.

Upholstery and Soft Furnishings

If it's been a while since you freshened up your upholstery and soft furnishings in the living room, you might want to take care of it this week.

Pop washable blankets, throws and cushion covers in the wash.

Vacuum and spot clean your fabric upholstery. Remove washable sofa covers or seat pads and pop them in the wash. See what you can find down the sides and under your seat pads! Washing your sofa covers may not be required at every zone clean so make a note on your checklist when you do it.

Use appropriate cleaners and cloths for leather upholstery to remove marks and condition the leather.

Small rugs can be taken outside and given a good shake before vacuuming, to freshen them up.

Doors & Woodwork

Doors and woodwork can be cleaned simply with warm soapy water and a clean cloth. A microfibre cloth will trap the dirt easily and leave the surface streak free. If you have glass panels in your doors, a microfibre cloth with warm water and a tiny dash of dishwashing detergent will work well. Polish off with a dry glass cleaning cloth to leave a sparkling shine! Don't forget the door frames, tops and edges of doors, hinges and handles. Scuff marks can be removed easily from painted doors with a well known miracle cleaning paste. Check on an inconspicuous area first though because it's abrasive!

If your skirting boards are dusty, vacuum first and then wipe down with a damp cloth.

Fireplace

Move everything away from the hearth area and protect your floor with plastic sheeting or old bed sheets. This can be a dirty job!

Next, remove the grate and clean it by wiping down with a damp microfibre cloth and patting it dry with an old towel.

Then, remove as much debris and ash as possible. If there is a lot, gently use a brush and shovel to remove the worst of it then use damp kitchen paper to pick up the rest. Clean the area thoroughly with warm soapy water and a damp cloth. rinsing well and leaving to air dry.

If your fireplace gets frequent use, it's a good idea to have the chimney inspected annually.

Floor

Do an extra thorough vacuuming this week, moving furniture aside where possible and getting under and behind it. Move couches and chairs, coffee tables, long curtains, pet beds, occasional tables, small units and plants. Mop hard floors.

ZONE 4
Dining Room or Home Office

Surface declutter

Cabinet/drawer declutter

Ceiling, walls & lighting

Windows/window treatments

Doors & Woodwork

Fireplace

Table & chairs / desk

Floor

Seasonal Zone Clean
Week 4: Dining Room/Home Office

If you have both a dining room and home office, see where you think your efforts should go. Either pick one this time and do the other next time or if they are both fairly tidy and clutter free already, you might manage both at the same time. If you don't have a dining room or home office you could catch up with any, tasks you didn't manage from zones 1-3, tackle a room of your choice or take the week off!

Surface Declutter
Look at your dining room or home office as if you were a visitor.
Where are the problem areas?
Does it look too busy?
How does it make you feel?
Think about how you want it to look and feel.

Is there anything you no longer use taking up valuable space
that you could get rid of?

Look for things that don't belong and for items that are preventing the space being used as it is intended.

One major thing to consider when decluttering any space is whether the room is functioning as it should. Are you able to have family meals or guests for dinner in your dining room or does the thought of it fill you with dread because the room isn't the way you want it?

Is your office a pleasant, inspiring work space? What could you do that would allow these things to happen? Maybe it's time for a change.

Remove unnecessary items from the table/desk, cabinets, shelves and floor. This is just a clearing and tidying job, no cleaning required.

Bag up anything for donation.
Relocate items to their proper home.
Recycle what you can.
Bin anything that can't be saved.

Cabinet or Drawer Declutter

Is there a cabinet, drawer or shelf in your dining room or home office in need of a sort out? Now is the perfect time.

Empty it. Sort through the contents and declutter. Categorise and organise the items you love, use and need and return them to the space in a way that makes you happy.

Use small boxes and lids to create compartments within drawers and on shelves. This will help to keep the space tidy and organised.

Ceiling, Walls & Lighting

This only needs done once or twice a year, so keep a note on your checklist when you do it.

Dust ceilings and walls using a long handled fluffy duster, a microfibre cloth or pillowcase on the end of a broom or your vacuum cleaner tools.

Start at the top and work your way down, going right into the corners. Get rid of cobwebs and be careful around lights.

Always work a room in the same order and it will help to create a system that makes the job easier and gives you less to think about.

For the lighting, warm soapy water and a well wrung out microfibre cloth should do the trick.

Microfibre cloths designed for cleaning glass are perfect for leaving glass fixtures and shades streak free.

A lint roller is perfect for removing dust from fabric lamp shades.

Seasonal Zone Clean
Week 4: Dining Room/Home Office

Windows & Window Treatments

If you want to keep your windows looking nice, it's a good idea to try to do them seasonally, every time the zone comes round.

Cleaning the inside of your windows every 3 months is manageable and will help prevent the dirt from building up too much.

For the windows, use your favourite window cleaning product or simply wash with warm water (with a tiny dash of dishwashing detergent in it) and a microfibre cloth.

A glass cleaning cloth will dry the window panes streak free and polish them off.

A lint roller is fantastic for removing dust from fabric blinds and curtains.

Doors & Woodwork

Doors and woodwork can be cleaned with warm soapy water and a clean cloth. A microfibre cloth will trap the dirt easily and leave the surface streak free.

If you have glass panels in your doors, a microfibre cloth with warm water and a dash of dishwashing detergent as above, will work well. Polish off with a dry lint free cloth. Don't forget the door frames, tops, edges, hinges and handles.

Scuff marks can be removed easily from painted doors with cleaning paste as before or a foam eraser. Always check on an inconspicuous area first as both are abrasive.

If your skirting boards are dusty, vacuum first, then wipe down with a damp cloth.

Upholstery & Soft Furnishings
There's probably not much in the way of upholstery and soft furnishings in these zones unless you have cushions or upholstered chairs. Pop any removable chair covers, blankets, throws and cushion covers in the wash. Vacuum and spot clean fabric upholstery. Use appropriate cleaners and cloths for leather upholstery to remove marks and condition the leather.

Fireplace
Move everything away from the hearth area and protect your floor with plastic sheeting or old bed sheets.

Remove the grate and clean it by wiping down with a damp microfibre cloth and patting it dry with an old towel. Remove as much debris and ash as possible. If there is a lot, gently use a brush and shovel to remove the worst of it then use damp kitchen paper to pick up the rest. Clean the area thoroughly with warm soapy water and a damp cloth. rinsing well and leaving to air dry.

If your fireplace gets frequent use, have the chimney inspected annually.

Floor
Do an extra thorough vacuuming this week, moving furniture aside where possible and getting under and behind it. Move chairs, small pieces of furniture, long curtains and large plants.

Use the soft brush attachment of the vacuum to dust around electrical equipment such as computer keyboard, monitor etc.

Take rugs outside where possible and give them a good shake.

Mop hard floors.

ZONE 5
Wardrobe Edit

Hanging Clothes

Folded Clothes

Shoes

Bags

Belts

Hats, Scarves, Gloves

Sunglasses

Watches

Jewellery

Seasonal Zone Clean
Week 5: Wardrobe Edit

Before you get started with editing your wardrobe, let's talk about how you can create your **dream wardrobe** - one where you love every item inside. The first step is visualisation. What do you want it to look like? Aim high and dream for a minute. Think...luxury boutique!

The experience you get in a boutique is all about how it makes you **feel**. The clothing is arranged beautifully. There is space between the hangers and the garments can breathe and move freely. Shoes and bags on display are seasonally appropriate and accessories laid out for selection. Lingerie is organised by colour and folded in neat little rows. Imagine if you could create that experience for yourself at home. The thing is, you can! And you don't need a huge walk-in closet or any money to achieve it. Knowing what you want is going to motivate you to declutter the unnecessary from your wardrobe.

Studies suggest that we only wear 20% of our clothing 80% of the time. Most of us would probably agree we have too much in our wardrobes, certainly more than we *need*. Consumerism and fast fashion plays a big part in this. Nowadays we live in a world of more, more, more. We want something, we get it! It feels exciting and thrilling when we see an item we love, decide to buy it and bring it home...to our already bulging wardrobe!

But what will happen if you keep doing this? Filling up your wardrobe is fun, in the beginning, but if you can't visually see what you own and you are not taking the time to regularly edit your belongings, you are creating a huge problem for yourself in the future. Your wardrobe becomes crammed with too many things, It looks squashed, wrinkled and unloved and you can't find anything. Not very inspiring when you want to get dressed in the morning and step outside, looking and feeling great. And I bet it's a million miles away from the picture you created in your mind of your dream wardrobe!

To solve the problem and work towards your dream wardrobe, you need to edit your belongings first and get rid of the items that no longer serve you. Be really honest with yourself as you go through the process. In addition, it's important to shop more mindfully going forward to break the clutter cycle and slow the influx of new belongings coming in. It can be life changing, when you take the time to edit and organise your wardrobe properly. You could even experiment with creating a capsule wardrobe. A small, carefully curated collection of clothing and accessories that mix and match to create lots of different outfits. Check out my blog on my website for further information on capsule wardrobe dressing (organisewithjen.com).

Challenges like Courtney Carver's Project 333 (bemorewithless.com) or The Ten-Item Wardrobe Concept (dailyconnoisseur.blogspot.com) can be a great way to learn more and experiment with this.

Some wardrobe tips before we begin editing;
Create a nice aesthetic
One way to create a beautiful, uniform, streamlined look in your wardrobe is to invest in matching hangers and coordinating containers for your accessories. My favourite type of hanger is the velvet, slimline design. They are space-saving and non-slip and come in lots of pretty colours and neutrals. Hanging your clothes on matching hangers will ensure all the garments hang neatly from the same height. It can be a big investment but you can do it in stages and build it up over time if you don't have the budget. Never buy storage for your wardrobe until after you've decluttered and always measure first.

Clothes you want to mend or sell
Keep clothes to mend and sell ONLY if there's a realistic chance you will do it. Piles of clothes waiting to be mended or listed are at risk of becoming clutter. The amount of time and energy it takes to sell is often disproportionate to the amount of money you will make. You have the choice. Give it away and you'll be free immediately, or if you do sell, put a short timeframe on it. List items within a week and after 2-4 weeks, donate anything left to avoid discarded items hanging around for months.

Seasonal Zone Clean
Week 5: Wardrobe Edit

In this zone, I'm taking you through the process of decluttering and organising your wardrobe. It's time to remove those items that no longer bring you joy and organise what's left to create a wardrobe full of pieces you truly love and feel excited to wear!

"Opening up your closet should be like arriving at a really good party, where everyone you see is someone you like." - Amy Fine Collins

One of my favourite wardrobe quotes! What a great analogy and reminder as you go through our wardrobe, deciding what should stay and what should go. It's safe to say the usual daily goal of 15-30 minutes may not apply to this task, especially if you're enjoying yourself! I don't know about you, but I love a good wardrobe declutter. This is my favourite zone!

The wardobe edit is week 5 of the programme for a reason. It's the ideal time in the new season to assess what's working and what's not. Not too early and not too late. I've broken the tasks down into manageable chunks to make it easier to tackle in sections over the course of the week.

If you struggle with letting go, ask yourself these questions as you handle each item;

Why do I have this?
Do I love it?
Do I wear it?
Do I need it?
Do I have anything else the same or similar?
Have I got at least three other things that go with it?
Will I need to buy something to go with it? Is that going to be worth it?

Does it make me look and feel my best?

The last question is probably the most important...if it's not an immediate yes, it's a probably a no and time to let it go.

HANGING CLOTHES

Begin the edit with the clothes that hang in your wardrobe or closet. If you have a large amount of clothing and it feels overwhelming, do one section of your wardrobe or one category of clothing at a time.

Remove the hanging clothes and sit them on the bed or floor in categories.

Your Hanging Clothing Categories may include...

Special Occasion Wear
Coats
Jackets
Gilets
Blazers
Suits
Maxi Dresses
Day Dresses
Maxi Skirts
Skirts
Trousers
Jeans
Hoodies

Long Cardigans
Short Cardigans
Chunky Knitwear
Fine Knitwear
Long Sleeved Tops
Short Sleeved T-shirts
Long Sleeved Shirts
Short Sleeved Shirts
Long Sleeved Blouses
Short Sleeved Blouses
Sleeveless Tops
Strappy Tops

Seasonal Zone Clean
Week 5: Wardrobe Edit

Give the inside of the wardrobe and the rail a quick clean and vacuum whilst it is empty. Now it's time to go through each category one item at a time. Hold each garment in your hand to assess how you feel about it. Keep only what you truly love and feel excited about wearing.

PEP TALK

I want you to ignore the silly rules you often hear regarding wardrobe decluttering such as, *'If you haven't worn it in 6 months or a year, get rid of it.'* This is simply not good advice! It's about how you **feel** about the item that's important, not how long you've had it.

With regards to making decisions about your clothes, here are some common decluttering stumbling blocks to be aware of;

It cost a fortune and you feel guilty that you never wear it.
The money's been spent and you had the pleasure of the thrill of the purchase when you bought it. Let it go and allow someone else to enjoy it.

You're hoping to fit into it one day.
At the risk of sounding harsh, stop putting your life on hold. The reality is, one day never comes. And if it does, you'll probably have changed your mind about the item by then anyway. You'll want to treat yourself to some new things to celebrate the new you. Having clothes taking up space in your wardrobe that don't fit, serves as a constant reminder that you're not happy with your body as it is. The garments will either drag you back to the past or depress you because they represent an idealised version of you in the future that you may never realise. If you can't wear them, why are they in your wardrobe? Release them from your life and dress for your body shape and the size you are right now.

If you simply love the fact you own something or get pleasure from looking at it, even if you won't wear it, find a way to honour its importance and store it where you can see it and enjoy it every day.

It was a gift.
The person who gave you the gift had the pleasure of selecting, purchasing and presenting the item to you.
Their job is done.

Your job is done too when you received the gift with gratitude.

Don't feel bad if you don't like it and don't write it off without giving it a chance. Take the tags off, experiment with it, use it, wear it, and if you still don't like it, donate it without guilt. You don't need to tell anyone or let it bother you. Only you know how you feel and it's your decision to make.

You might wear it one day.
You probably won't. One day never comes remember. There's a reason you're not wearing it. If you haven't worn it by now, you're not likely to.

Donate, sell or pass on without guilt.

Items you can say goodbye to include, anything stained, washed out, torn, bobbled, shrunk, stretched, shapeless and generally past its best. To keep them out of landfill, pop in a rag bag and donate or take to your local recycling centre.

Anything not wanted that's still in good condition, can be donated to charity. Make sure you bag up your discarded items and deal with them as soon as possible to avoid them making their way back into your wardrobe! Bin the rubbish immediately and put the donation bags in the car ready for your next trip into town.

REASONS TO KEEP AN ITEM OF CLOTHING...

- You LOVE it

- You WEAR it

- You NEED it

- It holds SPECIAL MEMORIES

- It makes you HAPPY

Okay, pep talk over. Let's go ahead and organise the clothing you are keeping.

Once you have sorted through your hanging clothes and gathered them in categories, you will see at a glance how many items you own within each one and how much space they will likely take up. Keep your garments in categories as you arrange them back on the rail and organise it in a way that feels right for you.

I hang my clothing in categories by length, longest to shortest, left to right. Coats and long dresses to the left, graduating to strappy tops at the right. Then within each category, by weight - heaviest to lightest, and also by colour - dark to light. This is the Konmari method made famous by Marie Kondo (konmari.com). I started using this method back in 2017 and have never looked back!

Some people prefer hanging their garments by colour, so if you fancy trying that, go ahead and create a rainbow. It's trial and error to see what works best for you.

Space on the rail is a must to allow the hangers to move and the clothes to breathe. The ultimate goal is to have a wardrobe that makes you smile and is a pleasure to go in everyday.

FOLDED CLOTHES

Next, let's focus on the folded clothes in your wardrobe or closet.

Any item of clothing can be folded, however some are better suited to folding than others. Fine, floaty fabrics are better suited to hanging to keep them crease free. Bulky garments are also best on a rail, due to their size.

The number of garments you can fold will also depend on the space you have available. Remove items from your drawers and shelves and sit them out on the bed or floor in categories.

If you have a large amount of folded clothing and it feels overwhelming, do one drawer or one category at a time.

Have bags ready for the items you will donate, pass on or sell.

Categories for folded clothing may include...

Lingerie & Shapewear
Nightwear
Socks & Hosiery
Activewear
Swimwear
Layering T-shirts
Regular T-shirts
Jeans
Hoodies
Chunky Knitwear

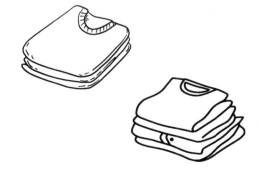

Seasonal Zone Clean
Week 5: Wardrobe Edit

Use the soft brush attachment to vacuum the inside of the empty drawers or shelves.

Wipe them with a clean damp cloth and allow to air dry while you sort through your clothing.

Hold each garment in your hand to assess how you feel about it.

KEEP ONLY WHAT YOU TRULY LOVE AND FEEL EXCITED ABOUT WEARING

When it comes to lingerie, socks and hosiery, really think about how many you actually need, based on how regularly you wash your clothes and how often you wear certain items.

This is a category that can easily multiply and get out of control.

Life is so much simpler when there is less choice and less to store.

Remember, don't keep an item of clothing because you might wear it one day. With the exception of special occasion wear, you probably won't.

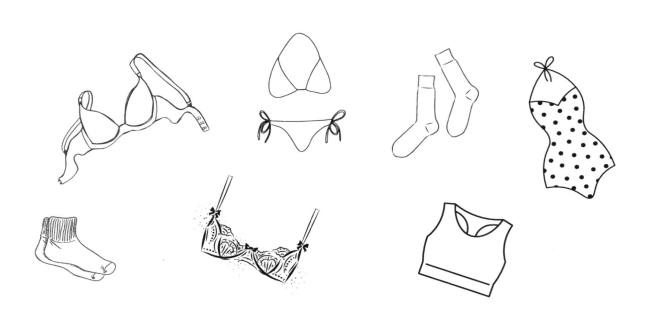

Let's talk about the science of folding. Yes! You read that right. There's something completely magical that happens when you fold your clothes in a way that makes everything visible, neat and visually appealing. A method that lasts and doesn't get destroyed the minute you take something out.

All my adult life, I thought I knew how to fold but I was in my mid-forties by the time I discovered **file folding** and now I don't know how I lived without it! Life is just a little bit more beautiful when you file fold and it is my preferred method for storing all clothes in drawers. In fact it goes beyond my wardrobe. Even my tea towels are file folded in my kitchen drawers!

If you're not familiar with file folding, it's where garments are folded into small rectangles and stored vertically like little files in a filing cabinet. To say it has been a total game changer for me and my clients, is an understatement and I can't recommend it highly enough. If you've not tried it yet, give it a go. It will bring an end to cluttered, chaotic drawers. No more crumpled clothes and no more time wasted searching for things!

When you fold and store this way, everything you own is visible to the eye and it works, I promise!

Here are some tips if you want to try it...

Use boxes and lids or expanding drawer dividers to create compartments. This stops the clothing falling over and keeps categories separate. You don't need to spend a fortune to get organised. Repurposing boxes you already have will work fine. Shoe boxes are the perfect size for t-shirts and nightwear. Small sturdy boxes that come with luxury socks, beauty products and candles are ideal for smaller items like hosiery and lingerie.

Ikea Skubb and Stuk boxes are a great option for organising drawers and wardobe shelves, if you have the budget.

Seasonal Zone Clean
Week 5: Wardrobe Edit

To create a system in your drawers that will keep everything organised, categorise your garments and store like with like.

Keep similar colours together within each category. Blacks then greys, then blues etc.

When everything has a home, it is so much easier to find what you are looking for and tidy things away.

Why not try a bit of ROY G BIV and rainbow order your folded clothes if you have lots of bright colours?

I like to organise my folded items with the same system I use with my hanging items, dark to light.

When folding your garments, aim to make the end product - the little rectangle - the same height as the depth of the box or drawer they will be stored in.

Avoid over stuffing drawers and cramming too many items into boxes.

They should ideally be around 90% full. Full enough for the items to hold each other up but also allow a little room for the clothes to breathe.

SHOES

Top tips for decluttering and organising your shoes.

Take them all out of the wardrobe and out of their boxes.

Clean as you go - the empty wardrobe and the shoes if they need it.

Keep every pair that you love, wear (even if it's just occasionally), fit you just now and you feel great in.

Try on any 'maybes' and be honest with yourself as you make your decisions.

First and foremost, let go of shoes and boots that are UNCOMFORTABLE! It's not worth the pain.

Get rid of shoes you never wear and any with holes, burst stitching, cracks and the ones you think you *might* wear one day... they can go.

Set aside any pairs you are keeping that need to visit the cobbler for new soles, heels or heel tips and take them soon!

Donate, sell or pass on any discarded pairs that are in good condition.

Shoes past their best and in poor condition can be binned, popped in a rag bag or taken to the recycling centre.

Organise the shoes you are keeping in categories such as ankle boots, knee high boots, ballet flats, mules, loafers, trainers, everyday heels, special occasion/evening shoes etc.

Seasonal Zone Clean
Week 5: Wardrobe Edit

Having shoes out on display looks lovely but if they're not worn regularly they will end up gathering dust. Something to consider if you have a walk-in wardrobe, dressing room or open closet.

Keep special occasion and evening shoes in their boxes to protect them and allow them to be stacked on a shelf.

Everyday shoes should be visible and easy to access, so you can see everything you own.

Be aware of how much space you have available and don't allow yourself to buy more than you can store. For storing and displaying your shoes, clear acrylic boxes, hanging shoe storage, shoe racks and shallow shelves are ideal. Shoe cabinets can be a stylish and ideal choice for a hallway to keep everyday shoes handy but out of sight.

Any out of season footwear can be stored separately in a box or storage bag until the seasons change again, if you don't have space for them in your current wardrobe.

BAGS

Are you a bag girl? How many do you have? How many do you need? Time to get your bags out to find out.

Sort through all your bags, categorising and removing any you know right away you can discard. Look at the condition of each bag and be honest with yourself as you decide which pile it belongs in - keep, donate, sell or rag bag.

Limit the space you have available for bags and you'll be less likely to overbuy and if you do bring a new one in, you can always edit your collection to make space for it. One in-one out.

One way to care for and store bags if you are short on space is to keep smaller bags inside larger bags. It saves space and can help to keep the shape of the larger bags. The only thing to note is that the smaller bags will not be visible, so try not to forget about them just because you can't see them.

A word on EVENING BAGS (before you declutter and get rid of any)

Accessories have the ability to make or break an outfit. The times in my life when I've most realised this was getting dressed up for a 'do' and discovering at the last minute I didn't have a suitable bag to wear. Panic!

Never underestimate the difference having the 'right' bag will make to your overall look. It adds a nice accent to your outfit whilst being practical at the same time. When you look good, you feel good.

Shape, style and colour are all you need to consider, along with quality if you want the bag to look good and have longevity.

Having the 'right' bag has nothing to do with how much it costs or which label is on it.

Seasonal Zone Clean
Week 5: Wardrobe Edit

When it comes to special occasion and evening bags, there are a few timeless styles to choose from. Frame bags, pouches, clutches, envelope clutches and minaudieres (hard case).

They will effortlessly complete any outfit and will be an investment you can rely on for years to come. You can't go wrong with a capsule collection of evening and special occasion bags in black, neutrals and metallics.

Evening bags don't take up too much room if you store them correctly. One way to do it is to stack them vertically in a shallow, lidded box. This is the method that's worked for me for years and I'd highly recommend it. It protects the bags from dust whilst also being easily accessible.

Embellished, designer or delicate bags will benefit from the extra protection of a dust bag. If you prefer your bags to be out on display, you could pop them in acrylic boxes or if you're prepared to put in the extra time and effort required to dust them, you could use acrylic dividers to help them stand up.

Do what feels right for you.

JEWELLERY AND WATCHES

If you struggle to keep your jewellery tidy and organised, I'd highly recommend having a good clear out and decluttering first before trying a new system or reorganising your jewellery in your existing system.

Most charity shops take donations of unwanted jewellery, even broken and damaged items, like odd earrings.

Organisers for jewellery and watches come in many shapes and sizes but I have to admit to being slightly obsessed with the stacking style made popular in recent years by the brand Stackers.

They can be set out flat inside a drawer or stacked up on a shelf or dressing table...so many options and very versatile.

They also come in a variety of colours and finishes to suit your taste. Leather, faux leather and velvet. I love how they keep the jewellery visible and organised and they look really pretty too. It's great being able to see all your jewellery at a glance. Goodbye tangled up necklaces and bracelets!

ACCESSORIES

Sort through all your cold and warm weather accessories, decluttering any you no longer need. Belts, sunglasses, scarves, hats, gloves, beachwear etc. Keep accessories handy that are appropriate for the current season. Out of season items are best categorised and stored in labelled containers that can be kept separate from your main wardrobe and brought back when the season comes round again. Either store in boxes at the top of your wardrobe if you have room, or pack away in a different wardrobe, cupboard, drawer or in boxes under your bed.

ZONE 6
Main Bedroom

Surface declutter

Cabinet/drawer declutter

Ceiling, walls & lighting

Windows/window treatments

Upholstery/soft furnishings

Doors & woodwork

Turn mattress/wash protectors

Floor

Seasonal Zone Clean
Week 6: Main Bedroom

Surface Declutter

It's a new zone so let's start with a surface declutter.
Look at your bedroom as though you were a visitor.
How does it make you feel?
Where are the problem areas?
Does it look too busy?

Think about how you want it to look and feel.

Is there anything you no longer use taking up valuable space and gathering dust that you could get rid of?

Could you remove any pieces of furniture?

Remove surface clutter from drawers, cabinets, shelves and floor.

This is just a clearing and tidying job today, not a cleaning job.

Bag up anything for donation.
Relocate items to their proper home.
Recycle what you can.
Bin what can't be saved.

Cabinet / Drawer Declutter

Is there a cabinet, drawer or shelf in your bedroom driving you mad?
How about your bedside table or nightstand?
Let's deal with it today.

Empty it. Sort through the contents and declutter. Categorise and organise the items you love, use and need in a way that makes sense for your lifestyle. Return them to the space. Use small boxes and lids to create compartments within drawers and on shelves. This will help to keep the space tidy and organised.

Ceiling, Walls & Lighting

This should only need done once or twice a year, so no need to do it if you did it last time. Make a note on your checklist when you do it so you can remember.

Dust ceilings and walls using a long handled fluffy duster, a pillowcase on the end of a broom or your vacuum cleaner tools. Start at the top and work your way down, going right into the corners. Move around your bedroom in a clockwise direction. Get rid of cobwebs and be careful around lights.

For the lighting, warm soapy water and a damp, well wrung out microfibre cloth should do the trick.

Microfibre cloths designed for cleaning glass are good for leaving glass fixtures and shades streak free. A lint roller will remove the dust from fabric shades easily.

Windows & Window Treatments

If you want to keep your windows looking good, it's a good idea to do them every time the zone comes round. Cleaning the inside of your windows every 3 months/every season, is manageable and will help prevent the dirt from building up too much.

For the windows, use your favourite window cleaner or simply wash with warm water (with a tiny dash of dishwashing detergent in it) and a microfibre cloth. Rinse well with clean water then use a glass cleaning cloth to dry and polish them off and make them sparkle!

Your soft brush attachment on your vacuum cleaner or a lint roller will remove dust easily from fabric blinds and curtains.

Seasonal Zone Clean
Week 6: Main Bedroom

Upholstery & Soft Furnishings

If it's been a while since you freshened up your upholstery and soft furnishings in the bedroom, you might want to tackle that this week as part of the zone clean. Pop blankets, throws and cushion covers in the wash.

Vacuum and spot clean fabric upholstery on chairs and headboard. Use appropriate cleaners and cloths for leather upholstery to remove marks and condition the leather.

Curtains can be vacuumed, steamed, dry cleaned or washed depending on the fabric and your preference - check labels.

Small rugs can be taken outside and given a good shake before vacuuming to freshen them up.

Doors & Woodwork

Doors and woodwork can be cleaned with warm soapy water and a clean cloth. A microfibre cloth will trap the dirt easily and leave the surface streak free.

If you have glass panels in your doors or furniture, a microfibre cloth with warm water and a dash of dishwashing detergent will work well. Polish off with a dry glass cleaning cloth to leave a sparkling shine! Don't forget the door frames, tops and edges of doors, hinges and handles. Scuff marks can be removed easily from painted doors with a magic eraser, cleaning paste or cream cleaner. There are a few on the market that are really good, but check on an inconspicuous area first because they're abrasive.

If your skirting boards are dusty, vacuum first, then wipe down with a damp cloth.

Turn Mattress & Wash Protectors

If you have a mattress that requires turning every so often, do it this week or the next time you change your sheets.

Pop your pillow and mattress protectors in the wash at 60 degrees along with your bed linen and dry outside if possible.

While the mattress is clear, vacuum it thoroughly using the small tool.

Floor

Do an extra thorough vacuuming this week, moving furniture aside where possible and getting under and behind it. Move chairs, small pieces of furniture, long curtains and large plants.

If you can't move the bed, move what's under it and vacuum what you can reach.

Use the soft brush attachment of your vacuum cleaner to dust along the edges and around cables. To remove the dust that the vacuum cleaner can't reach, rub hard along the edge of the carpet right against the skirting board with a damp cloth to dislodge it. Vacuum the debris up.

Take rugs outside where possible and give them a good shake.

Mop hard floors.

Seasonal Zone Clean
Week 6: Main Bedroom

Make-up

If you store your make-up in your bedroom, you may want to declutter and organise it this week as part of your bedroom zone clean.

Take all your make-up and brushes out and sort into categories.

Discard any make-up that you never use, is old, past it's best/possibly a health hazard (see below for how long make-up can be safely used) Make a note of anything you need to replace.

Discard old worn brushes with damaged or loose bristles; no one wants a hairy face! Wipe down palettes and the containers you keep your make-up in. Wash your brushes and leave to air dry. Clean your make-up bag or container. Enjoy organising your beautifully curated make-up collection!

Make-up Expiration

Here is a list of the recommended life expectancy of cosmetics and how long it is deemed safe to use them once they have been opened.

*Trust your nose, if something smells icky, don't use it!

- Powder formulas, mineral foundation, powder eye shadow and powder blush 2y
- Cream formula base products like foundation and concealer 1y
- Cream Formula eye shadow, cream blush, brow gel 6m
- Brow, eye & lip pencils 2y
- Mascara and liquid liner 3-6m
- Lipstick and stick lip balm 2y+
- Lip glosses and lip balms in pots 1y
- Nail polish 2y+ (if kept cool, in the dark, upright, with the lid on)
- Fragrance 8-10y+ (if kept cool, in the dark, with the lid on)

ZONE 7
Kid's Room or Guest Room

Surface declutter

Wardrobe/drawer declutter

Ceiling, walls & lighting

Windows/window treatments

Upholstery/soft furnishings

Doors & woodwork

Turn mattress/wash protectors

Floor

Seasonal Zone Clean
Week 7: Kids'/Guest Bedroom

Surface Declutter

In this zone, you are going to focus on your guest room, spare room or child's' room. If you have several rooms in this zone, pick ONE and focus on that this time. Next time do a different one...it's all about making it manageable. Which one will you do?

As always, let's start with a surface declutter.

Look at the room as though you were a visitor.
How does it make you feel?
Where are the problem areas?
Does it look too busy?
Think about how you want it to look and feel.
Is there anything you no longer use taking up valuable space and gathering dust?
Could you remove any pieces of furniture?

Remove surface clutter from drawers, cabinets, shelves and floor.

This is just a clearing and tidying job today, not a cleaning job.

Bag up anything for donation.
Relocate items to their proper home.
Recycle what you can.
Bin what can't be saved.

Drawer Declutter

Is there a cabinet, drawer or shelf in the room driving you mad? How about the bedside table, nightstand or desk?

Empty it. Sort through the contents and declutter.

Categorise and organise the items you are keeping and return them to the space if it makes sense to keep them there. Use small boxes and lids to create compartments within drawers and on shelves. This will help to keep the space tidy and organised.

Wardrobe Edit

Take some time to straighten up and sort your child's wardrobe or guest room wardobe/cupboard this week. Assess what's working well and what's not.

Like you did with your own wardrobe, start with the hanging clothes. Look through them on the rail. Remove anything that is no longer used, garments your child has outgrown and anything that won't be worn.

Next check the drawers.
Empty them and do the same.
Keep like with like.
Categorise and organise.
Fold and arrange back in the drawer, storing vertically where possible. Use drawer dividers or old shoe boxes to create compartments within the drawer.

If there is a wardrobe in your guest room, check that it is guest ready with everyday essentials and items they may have forgotten to pack... toothbrush, tissues, spare pillows, blankets etc.

Ceiling, Walls & Lighting

This should only need done once or twice a year, so no need to do it if you did it last time. Make a note on your checklist so you can remember.

Dust ceilings and walls using a long handled fluffy duster, a microfibre cloth or pillowcase on the end of a broom or your vacuum cleaner tools. Start at the top and work your way down, going right into the corners. Move around the room in a clockwise direction. Get rid of cobwebs and be careful around lights.

For the lighting, use warm soapy water and a damp, well wrung out microfibre cloth.

Microfibre cloths designed for cleaning glass are good for leaving glass fixtures and shades streak free. A lint roller is fantastic for removing dust from fabric shades.

Windows & Window Treatments

If you want to keep the windows looking good, it's a good idea to do them every time the zone comes round.

Cleaning the inside of your windows every 3 months is manageable and will help prevent the dirt from building up too much.

For the windows, use your favourite window cleaning product or simply wash with warm water (with a tiny dash of dishwashing detergent mixed in) and a microfibre cloth.

A glass cleaning cloth will dry and polish them off and make them sparkle!

Your soft brush attachment on your vacuum cleaner or a lint roller will easily remove dust from fabric blinds and curtains.

Upholstery & Soft Furnishings

If it's been a while since you freshened up the upholstery and soft furnishings in the guest room or your child's room, you might want to tackle that this week as part of the zone clean. Pop blankets, throws and cushion covers in the wash.

Vacuum and spot clean fabric upholstery on chairs and headboard. Use appropriate cleaners and cloths for leather upholstery to remove marks and condition the leather.

Curtains can be vacuumed, steamed, dry cleaned or washed depending on the fabric and your preference - check labels.

Small rugs can be taken outside and given a good shake before vacuuming to freshen them up.

Doors and Woodwork

Doors and woodwork can be cleaned with warm soapy water and a clean cloth. A microfibre cloth will trap the dirt easily and leave the surface streak free.

If you have glass panels in your doors or furniture, a microfibre cloth with warm water and a dash of dishwashing detergent will work well. Polish off with a dry glass cleaning cloth to leave a sparkling shine! Don't forget the door frames, tops and edges of doors, hinges and handles.

Scuff marks can be removed easily from painted doors with a magic eraser, cleaning paste or cream cleaner. Check on an inconspicuous area first.

If your skirting boards are dusty, vacuum first, then wipe down with a damp cloth.

Seasonal Zone Clean
Week 7: Kids'/Guest Bedroom

Turn Mattress & Wash Protectors

If the mattress requires regular turning, do it this week or the next time you change the sheets.

(Probably not necessary for a rarely used guest bed.)

Pop pillow and mattress protectors in the wash along with the bed linen and dry outside if possible. Hoover the mattress whilst it is airing.

For guest rooms, it's important to launder the protectors and bedding a few days before your guests arrive, so it is not only clean but smells fresh too. Bedding that has been stored unused for any length of time can start to smell musty.

Floor

Do an extra thorough vacuuming this week, moving furniture aside where possible, getting under and in behind it.

Move chairs, small pieces of furniture, long curtains and large plants.

If you can't move the bed, move what's under it and vacuum what you can reach.

Use the crevice tool of your vacuum cleaner to dust along the edges and around cables. Use a damp cloth wrapped around your finger to rub along the edge of the carpet where it meets the skirting board. This will dislodge any dust the vacuum cleaner can't reach. Vacuum up the debris that comes out.

Take rugs outside where possible and give them a good shake.

Mop hard floors.

ZONE 8
The Bathroom

Surface declutter

Cabinet/drawer declutter

Ceiling, walls & lighting

Windows / window treatments

Doors & woodwork

Tiles & grout

Shower

Sink Unit

(Make-Up)

Seasonal Zone Clean
Week 8: Bathroom

Surface Declutter

If you have multiple bathrooms in your home, it may be best to pick just one to focus on this time and do a different one next time. Look to see which one needs the most attention and start there. It's up to you! Start the new zone with a surface declutter.

Look at your bathroom as though you were a visitor. How does it make you feel? Where are the problem areas? Think about how you want it to look and feel.

Are there lots of products cluttering up the space that you could use up quickly and get rid of? Any duplicates? Is your bathroom difficult to clean because there are too many things out on display? Bottles, decor, plants, toys. Do you have adequate storage?

For starters remove all surface clutter and try to store as much as possible out of sight. Clear surfaces will make your bathroom feel calmer and much easier to clean.

Prioritise products you want to use up soon.
Relocate items to their proper home.
Recycle what you can.
Bin anything that can't be saved.

Cabinet/Drawer Declutter

Is there a cabinet, drawer or shelf in your bathroom driving you mad? Let's tackle it today? Empty it. Sort through the contents and declutter.

Categorise the items you love, use and need and return them to the space, keeping like with like. Give everything a home that makes sense.

Use small boxes and lids to create compartments within drawers and on shelves. This will help to keep the space tidy and organised.

Ceiling, Walls & Lighting

This should only need done once or twice a year, so no need to do it if you did it last time. Make a note on your checklist when you do it.

Dust ceilings and walls using a long handled fluffy duster, a microfibre cloth or pillowcase on the end of a broom or your vacuum cleaner tools. Start at the top and work your way down, going right into the corners. Move around the zone in a clockwise direction. Get rid of cobwebs and be careful around lights. Panelled bathroom ceilings can be wiped with a microfibre cloth and warm water, if you can reach it!

For the lighting, warm soapy water and a damp, well wrung out microfibre cloth should do the trick.

Microfibre cloths designed for cleaning glass are good for leaving glass fixtures and shades streak free.

A lint roller will remove dust from fabric shades.

Windows & Window Treatments

If you want to keep your windows looking good, it's a good idea to try to do them every time the zone comes round. Cleaning the inside of your windows every 3 months is manageable and will help prevent the dirt from building up too much.

For the windows, use your favourite window cleaning product or simply wash with warm water (with a tiny dash of dishwashing detergent in it) and a microfibre cloth. A glass cleaning cloth will dry and polish them off and make them sparkle!

Depending on material, blinds can be vacuumed with the soft brush attachment of your hoover or dusted with a lint roller, then wiped with a damp microfibre cloth.

Seasonal Zone Clean
Week 8: Bathroom

Doors & Woodwork

Doors and woodwork can be cleaned with warm soapy water and a clean cloth. A microfibre cloth will trap the dirt easily and leave the surface streak free.

Don't forget the door frames, tops and edges of doors, hinges and handles.

Scuff marks can be removed easily from painted doors with a magic eraser, cleaning paste or a cream cleaner. Check on an inconspicuous area first.

If your skirting boards, tiles or panelling are dusty, vacuum first, then wipe down with a damp cloth.

Tiles & Grout

If you have tiles or wet wall panels, wipe them down with warm soapy water and a microfibre cloth or your favourite bathroom cleaner.

If the surface is rough, uneven or bumpy, you might prefer to use a small brush or an old toothbrush to remove dust, staining, mould and mildew.

Grout can be freshened up and whitened with a drop of bleach on the bristles of an old toothbrush - *be careful though and do your research, this is NOT suitable for all tiles and will depend on what material they are made from. Bleach is strong and can dull and strip some glossy, porous or shiny surfaces, so it's best to test first on an inconspicuous area.

A cleaning paste might be another option if bleach is too strong, but always best to test first. If you are on the market for a new bathroom, choosing grey or beige grout can be a good choice that will give you less work in the future.

Shower & Sink

My number 1 tip for cleaning your shower and bathroom is to clean it while you're in it!

So much easier when there is moisture in the air and you have a microfibre cloth in your hand! If you take a few minutes to rinse your shower down after use and dry it off with a microfibre cloth, you'll never have to actually *clean* it. Honestly! I've been using this method for over a decade and it's the only thing that truly works. Prevention is better than cure. Keep a microfibre cloth hanging over the shower screen so it is handy and easy to grab. Hang it to dry between times and wash it in the machine once or twice a week, along with your regular load.

The shower hose and plughole and trap will benefit from a scrub with an old toothbrush once a month if you really want to keep on top of it, but once each zone clean provides a good baseline.

Treat your sink, taps and plughole to an extra thorough clean this week.

To freshen plugholes and drains, pour down a cup of soda crystals or baking soda. Leave for 15-20 minutes before flushing down with hot water. It will remove nasty smells and clear away gunk and slime.

Make-up

If you store your make-up in your bathroom, you may want to declutter and organise it this week as part of your bathroom zone clean.

Refer back to Zone 6 Main Bedroom for information and tips on this.

ZONE 9
Hall and Entryway

Surface declutter

Cabinet/drawer declutter

Ceiling, walls & lighting

Windows / window treatments

Banister

Doors & woodwork

Front door

Entryway

Floor

Seasonal Zone Clean
Week 9: Hall & Entryway

Surface Declutter

This is a very important space in the home. The first place you see when you walk in the front door. It's important to get it right and create a good first impression, not just for guests, but for you and your family too. Think about how you can make it feel warm and welcoming. Sart as always with a quick assessment and surface declutter. Stand at your front door as though you were a visitor.

What do you see?
How does it make you feel?
Is it welcoming?
What's working well and what's not?
Think about how you want it to look and feel.

Is there anything cluttering up the space that doesn't belong?

Is there adequate storage for keys/mail/coats/shoes etc?

Remove all clutter from the floor and surfaces. Clear surfaces will make your entryway calmer, more inviting and much easier to clean.
Get rid of anything you don't use/don't like/don't need anymore.

Bag up anything for donation.
Relocate items to their proper home.
Recycle what you can.
Bin what can't be saved.

Cabinet/Drawer Declutter

Is there a cabinet, drawer or shelf in your entrance vestibule, hall or landing driving you mad? Let's deal with it today. Empty it. Sort through the contents and declutter. Remove what doesn't belong. Relocate items to their proper home. Categorise and organise the things you love, use and need and return them to the space. Use small boxes and lids to create compartments within drawers and on shelves. This will help to keep the space tidy and organised.

Ceiling, Walls & Lighting

This should only need done once or twice a year, so no need to do it if you did it last time.

Dust ceilings and walls using a long handled fluffy duster, a microfibre cloth or pillowcase on the end of a broom or your vacuum cleaner tools. Start at the top and work your way down, going right into the corners. Move around the zone in a clockwise direction. Get rid of cobwebs and be careful around lights.

For the lighting, warm soapy water and a damp, well wrung out microfibre cloth should be enough. Microfibre cloths designed for cleaning glass are good for leaving glass fixtures and shades streak free.

A lint roller will remove dust from fabric shades.

Windows & Window treatments

To keep your windows looking good, try to do them every time the zone comes round. It will help prevent the dirt from building up too much.

Glass on the front door, picture frames and wall mirrors can be done today, but will benefit from more regular cleaning between times also. For the glass, use your favourite window cleaning product or simply wash with warm water (with a tiny dash of dishwashing detergent in it) and a glass cleaning microfibre cloth. A regular microfibre cloth will be fine for the frames and vents. A dry glass cleaning cloth will polish all your glass to a streak free finish.

Depending on material, blinds can be vacuumed, dusted with a lint roller or wiped with a damp microfibre cloth. If your curtains are washable, they will only need done once per year.

Seasonal Zone Clean
Week 9: Hall & Entryway

Banister, Doors & Woodwork

If you have a banister, start at the top and work your way down, cleaning the hand rail, glass or spindles with warm soapy water and a microfibre cloth. Repeat with the doors and woodwork. A microfibre cloth will trap the dirt easily and leave the surface streak free.

Don't forget the door frames, tops, edges, hinges and handles.
Scuff marks can be removed easily from painted doors with a magic eraser, cleaning paste or cream cleaner. Check on an inconspicuous area. If your skirting boards or panelling are dusty, vacuum first, before wiping down with a damp cloth.

Front Door & Entryway

Give the front door some extra TLC this week. Clean the interior first, then the exterior. Warm soapy water and a couple of microfibre cloths to wash and dry, should do the job perfectly.

Vacuum the threshold with the crevice tool to remove dust and debris from the grooves and wipe the bottom ledge with a damp cloth. Tidy up the area just outside, pulling weeds, shaking mats and sweeping if necessary. You might want to add a few seasonal pots or a wreath to your front door to brighten up the space and make it feel extra welcoming.

Floor

If you have any freestanding furniture in your hall or landing or have removable radiator covers, move them out and vacuum under and behind them this week.

A damp cloth pulled along the edge of your carpet where it meets the skirting board will pick up the dust that the vacuum cleaner often misses.

Vacuum the stairs and landing.
Shake rugs outside.
Mop hard floors.

ZONE 10
Utility Room/Laundry Room

Surface declutter

Cabinet/drawer declutter

Ceiling, walls & lighting

Windows / window treatments

Doors & woodwork

Cupboards & drawer fronts

Washing machine

Tumble dryer

Sink unit

Floor

Seasonal Zone Clean
Week 10: Utility/Laundry Room

Surface Declutter

If your home doesn't have a utility room or laundry room, you could take the week off or you could do a room you haven't covered, such as family room, playroom, extension, spare room etc.

Let's get started with a surface declutter.
Look at the room with a fresh pair of eyes, as though you were a visitor.
How does it make you feel?
Is it serving its purpose and functioning as it should?
Does it look too busy?
Even though it is a functional space, think about how you want it to look and feel.
Is there anything you no longer use taking up valuable space and gathering dust that you could get rid of?

Remove surface clutter from shelves, counter tops, and floor.

This is a clearing and tidying job today, not a cleaning job.

Bag up anything for donation.
Relocate items to their proper home.
Recycle what you can.
Bin what can't be saved.

Cabinet/Drawer Declutter

Is there a cabinet or drawer in your utility/laundry room driving you mad? Let's deal with it today?

Empty it. Sort through the contents and declutter. Check for duplicates of cleaning products or too many different products that all do the same job. Relocate items to their proper home. Categorise and organise the items you use and need and return them to the space. Use containers or turntables to store the items you are keeping and to help you create a manageable system where everything has a home. This will help to keep the space tidy and organised.

Ceiling, Walls & Lighting

This should only need done once or twice a year, so no need to do it if you did it last time. Make a note on your checklist so you remember when you did it.

Dust ceilings and walls using a long handled fluffy duster, a microfibre cloth or pillowcase on the end of a broom or your vacuum cleaner tools. Start at the top and work your way down, going right into the corners. Move around the zone in a clockwise direction. Get rid of cobwebs and be careful around lights.

For the lighting, warm soapy water and a damp, well wrung out microfibre cloth should do the job well.

Microfibre cloths designed for cleaning glass are great for leaving glass fixtures and shades streak free.

A lint roller will remove dust from fabric shades easily.

Windows & Window Treatments

To keep your windows looking nice, it's a good idea to try to do them every time the zone comes round. It will help prevent the dirt from building up too much. If you have glass in your doors, they can be done this week too but will benefit from more regular cleaning between times also.

For the glass, use your favourite window cleaning product or simply wash with warm water (with a tiny dash of dishwashing detergent in it) and a glass cleaning microfibre cloth. A regular microfibre cloth will be fine for the frames and vents.

A dry lint free cloth will polish all your glass to a streak free finish. Depending on material, blinds can be vacuumed, dusted with a lint roller or wiped with a damp microfibre cloth.

Seasonal Zone Clean
Week 10: Utility/Laundry Room

Doors & Woodwork

Doors both interior and exterior, if this zone has one, and the woodwork, can be cleaned with warm soapy water and a microfibre cloth. It will trap the dirt easily and leave the surface streak free.

If you have glass panels in your doors, warm water and a dash of dishwashing detergent will work well. Polish off with a dry glass cleaning cloth to leave a sparkling shine!

Don't forget the door frames, tops and edges of doors, hinges and handles. Scuff marks can be removed easily from painted doors with a magic eraser, cleaning paste or a cream cleaner.
Check on an inconspicuous area first as the latter two are abrasive.

If your skirting boards are dusty, vacuum first, then wipe down with a damp cloth.

Cupboard & Drawer Fronts

This task shouldn't take long at all. A cloth and warm soapy water should be all you need to clean the cupboard and drawer fronts and any shelving. A microfibre cloth will work with water alone to trap the dirt easily and leave the surface streak free.

If it has been a while however, and dirt and grime have built up, you may prefer to use a multi-purpose kitchen spray, a degreaser or a cream cleaner instead. Avoid scrubbing cream cleaner on glossy finishes as it could dull the shine.

Washing Machine Tips

If your washing machine detergent drawer is in need of a good scrub, remove it completely and wash thoroughly in warm, soapy water. Don't forget to clean the cavity too. Spray a multi-purpose cleaning product into the cavity and leave it to work its magic for 5 minutes while you clean the detergent drawer. Scrub the cavity with an old toothbrush and a microfibre cloth. Rinse well and put it all back together.

To maintain it going forward, keep a dry microfibre cloth handy in your utility room just for your washing machine and spend a minute wiping the drawer, door and rubber gasket after your load of laundry is removed each wash day. This will soak up any residual water and prevent, bacteria, mould and mildew forming. Keep the door and drawer slightly open at all times to allow air to circulate between washes.

It's a good idea to run a maintenance wash once a month to kill bacteria and keep mould, mildew and nasty odours at bay. Simply run your washing machine empty on the longest, hottest cycle. Use biological powder (no softener). The enzymes present in bio powder have germ killing properties and will give your machine a really good clean.

If you prefer a more natural method, pop a cup of baking soda in the detergent drawer and a cup of white vinegar in the drum and run the hottest, longest cycle.

Seasonal Zone Clean
Week 10: Utility/Laundry Room

Tumble Dryer Tips
A few tips to keep your tumble dryer clean and in good working order...

Empty the water tank every time you use it.

Remove fluff from the lint filter after every use. This will keep your machine running safely and efficiently. Forgetting to do this can be a potentially dangerous fire hazard due to build up of heat. If you have a wall vent, check it is clear of fluff too.

Clean the inside of the drum and drying sensor by wiping with a cloth and multi-purpose cleaner.

Rinse the heat exchanger under the tap regularly to remove clogged, dirty fibres.

Sink Unit
Remove everything from the countertop, cleaning items as you go. Wipe it down thoroughly.

Empty the under sink cupboard and declutter. Look for duplicates and products you can use up quickly. Wash the interior and leave to dry while you sort out and categorise the items you want to keep.

Before you put everything back, give the sink and splashback a good scrub paying particular attention to the taps and plug hole.

To clean and freshen the drain, pop a cup of soda crystals down the plug hole, leave for 15-20 minutes, then flush away with hot water.

Reorganise the under sink cupboard with only the items you need and use regularly.

ZONE 11
Choose:

Walk-in/Built-in Cupboard

Hobby Room

Household Paperwork & Filing

Digital Declutter

Seasonal Zone Clean
Week 11: You Choose

You're almost there! Welcome to Week 11, the penultimate week and the second last zone of the seasonal programme.

If you have a large built-in or walk-in cupboard in need of a sort out, you could dedicate this week to doing it. Tackle it in stages if it feels too much to empty it all in one go. Ensure you have a clear space to work and plenty of room to arrange the items. Categorise everything that comes out and declutter the things that no longer serve you. That's the only way to see what you've got and create a new organised system that will work for you long term.

If there is a room in your home that you didn't get to or that we haven't covered, such as a family room, playroom, hobby room, extension, conservatory, spare room...this could be the week for it! Refer back to the zone you missed or choose a similar zone, check the list and pick from the suggested tasks.

If you missed Zone 5 Wardrobe Edit, you could spend this week doing that.

If you're ready for something different but also necessary (that doesn't involve cleaning), you could deal with your household paperwork or do a digital clutter this week. The next few pages will walk you through the process...

PAPERWORK & FILING

Seasonal Zone Clean
Week 11: Paperwork

Okay let's start with household paperwork!

Letters, junk mail, newspapers, magazines, bills, catalogues, instruction manuals, store leaflets, brochures, medical notes, takeaway menus, appointments, policies, certificates, kids' artwork, school correspondence, important documents... have I forgotten anything?

We will DECLUTTER, CATEGORISE and ORGANISE...

Mail

Receipts

Magazines, Leaflets, Catalogues

Personal Documents

Household Paperwork

Bills

School/Work/Business Correspondence

DECLUTTER * CATEGORISE * ORGANISE

Day 1: Mail

- Have a paper recycling bin handy and a shredder if you have one.

- Gather all the mail together and go through it one item at a time.

- Put junk mail straight into the paper bin, tearing off any name/address details and shredding those as you go.

- Organise anything important into two piles.

1. Filing
2. Needs attention

File straight away and deal with your 'needs attention' pile as soon as you can.

Seasonal Zone Clean
Week 11: Paperwork

DECLUTTER * CATEGORISE * ORGANISE

Day 2: Receipts

- Have a paper recycling bin handy and a shredder if you have one.

- An expanding file, labelled Jan-Dec is my favourite way to organise and store receipts. So simple!

- Empty your purse and bag and gather all your receipts together in one spot.

- Check them one at a time, look at the date and file accordingly in the correct pocket for that month.

- Bin receipts older than one year unless they belong to something with a guarantee or warranty longer than a year. Keep those in the front pocket of your file.

- Keep an envelope in the December pocket labelled specifically for Christmas gift receipts.

- Voila! Never lose a receipt again!

Week 11: Paperwork

DECLUTTER * CATEGORISE * ORGANISE

Day 3: Magazines, Leaflets, Catalogues

- Have a recycling bin handy and find a clear space with a large flat surface to work on. A table or the floor is perfect.

- Magazines, catalogues and leaflets have a habit of multiplying and spreading to every room in the house, so start by gathering them all together in one spot and separate into the 3 categories. Now you have them all in one spot, you will see clearly how many you own. If you have an overwhelming amount to deal with, break it up and do one pile at a time in any one sitting.

- Start with the smallest pile and aim to eliminate it first. Keep only what you intend to read or browse and discard the rest.

- Move on to the next pile and aim to eliminate it completely or at least reduce it. Keep only what you love, use, need and discard the rest.

- Tackle the largest pile in the same way, going through each item one at a time, discarding what no longer serves you.

- Glossy magazines can be donated to charity shops. Limited edition or special edition magazines might be worth keeping but if you want to let them go, they may sell on eBay or Amazon Marketplace. It's worth doing your research if you have the time.

Finally, don't forget the GOLDEN RULE...As tempting as it may be, never get rid of anyone else's stuff! Decluttering and organising is infectious. Once family members see the positive impact it's having on you, your life and your home, they'll most likely be inspired to give it a go too. We live in hope!

Seasonal Zone Clean
Week 11: Paperwork

DECLUTTER * CATEGORISE * ORGANISE

Day 4: Personal Documents

Everyone needs a place to keep their own personal keepsakes and memorabilia as well as a place to keep personal documents.
Birth certificate, school reports, certificates of achievement, medical notes, childhood drawings, favourite cuddly toy, personal writing, exam results...

To organise this category effectively, it's important that each family member has an individual keepsake bin or memory box, plus a binder or file in which to keep personal documents and paperwork. Labelled poly pockets within the file will keep everything super organised!

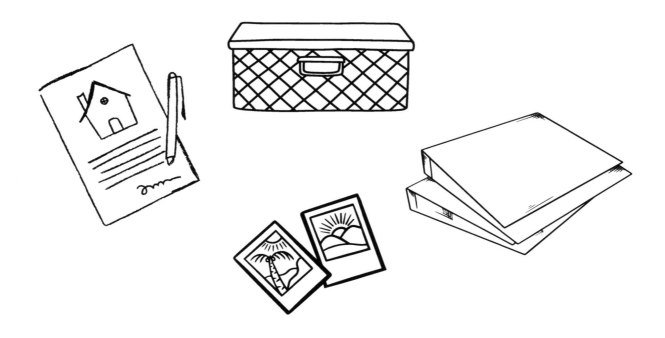

DECLUTTER * CATEGORISE * ORGANISE

Day 4: Personal Documents

Now you have a place to put things, you can begin to sort through the paperwork and file accordingly, ensuring everything has a home.
Keep the things that truly matter to you and hold a special place in your heart. No one else can tell you what those things are, only you will know. If it 'sparks joy' it's a keeper!

Discard unnecessary papers and personal paperwork that you didn't even remember you had. Let go of papers that don't matter to you anymore or that you no longer need to hold onto.

Shred anything containing personal details and sensitive information and pop everything else in the paper recycle bin.

If you have an excessive amount of paper that needs shredded, there are businesses that offer this service for you, even if it's confidential paperwork. Sometimes it's worth paying the experts to get the job done quickly, in order to be free of the physical and mental burden immediately.

Seasonal Zone Clean
Week 11:
Paperwork & Filing

DECLUTTER * CATEGORISE * ORGANISE

Day 5:
Household Paperwork, Bills, School Correspondence

Whether you have a little or a lot, household paperwork can get out of control very easily. To tame this category of paperwork, you need to first of all gather it together in one clear space and categorise everything into piles, like with like.

Declutter and shred as you go and you'll visibly see how much you have within each category that you need to keep.

Take the time to switch and go paper-free where possible, especially with bills and you will drastically reduce the amount of paper coming into your home.

A ring binder for each category should suffice, plus I'd recommend an everyday homefile and a file for important documents like birth/marriage certificates, wills, power of attorney, title deeds etc.

This is a suggestion and what has worked well for me and my family for years. It might work for you too or you may need to tweak it to suit.

Next, you'll see a rundown of my household file categories and examples of what I keep in them...

DECLUTTER * CATEGORISE * ORGANISE

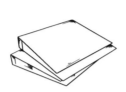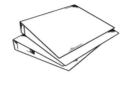

HOUSEHOLD FILES

There is a file for each family member containing their medical and personal info, school reports, achievements etc.
In addition to this we have...

File 1: HOME
A place to store mortgage docs, insurance, valuation certificates, utilities, council tax, home improvements info etc.

File 2: CAR
A place to store all papers related to the cars, insurance, road tax, mot, repairs, vehicle purchase documents etc.

File 3: MONEY
A place to store all papers related to personal and household finances, Bank Accounts, Savings Accounts, ISAs, Savings Plans, Life Insurance, Payslips, P60s, tax info etc.

IMPORTANT DOCS (a flat envelope file)
Birth/marriage certificates, legal docs, power of attorney, house title deeds etc.
EVERYDAY HOME FILE (an expanding file with labelled pockets)
Appointment letters, vouchers, tickets, travel docs, passports, school correspondence, take-away menus etc.

DIGITAL DECLUTTER

1 - EMAILS

Whether you have one email address or multiple, this can be a very time consuming and overwhelming job. I'm not suggesting you clear out the whole lot in one go. Make it easy and focus on what feels manageable to you today...one week's worth maybe, or last month's emails, work emails, personal emails, marketing and junk emails. You decide.

The secret to keeping on top of a large inbox is reducing what's coming in in the first instance by unsubscribing to companies you would rather not hear from. Secondly, edit regularly - daily, weekly, bimonthly or monthly and that will help enormously in keeping it manageable and under control.

Let's get started. Set yourself a timer for 15, 20 or 30 minutes and sit down with a cup of tea or something nice. Have a look at your inbox and decide where to begin. Delete your most recent emails straight away that you know you don't need.

Use the search bar to find specific emails and move them to the recycle bin or archive if you want to keep them. Delete in bulk where possible rather than individually. I find this easier on the laptop than my mobile.

To stop new emails coming from companies you no longer want to hear from, type UNSUBSCRIBE into the search bar and it will bring up all the business emails with that option. Go ahead and unsubscribe. You'll still need to delete past emails but at least no new ones will come.

Seasonal Zone Clean
Week 11: Digital Declutter

2 - SMARTPHONE APPS / HOME SCREEN

It's time to check through, declutter and streamline the apps you have built up on your phone home screen. If you're anything like me, that's quite a few, and you might not be using them all!

Go for the quick wins first. Delete the apps you see straight away that you know you don't need. If you don't recognise an app or know what it is for or remember why you downloaded it, it can probably go.

Secondly, go into your general settings and look at phone storage. Check the list to see how much space your apps are individually taking up and delete the ones you can do without.

Create folders for your apps to keep your home screen tidy and organised. This can be done by type or colour. Organising by type is easier and makes complete sense straight away. Organising by colour looks more aesthetically pleasing but takes a bit of getting used to! You really need to know your app colours and company logos for this to work and be user-friendly. I love having my phone home screen organised like this but I hated it at first. It took 2-3 days to retrain my brain and enjoy the new system.

Finally go to your settings and check your subscriptions to make sure you're not paying for anything you don't use. You can cancel subscriptions whilst they are active if you know you won't be renewing them. They will still remain active until the renewal date.

3 - PHONE CAMERA ROLL

Lets's start easy with checking through all the pics freshest in your memory that you took on your phone last month.

Delete images straight away that you know you don't need.

If you have holiday pics or attended a special event it's wise to create an album in your photo app to save them in. That way you'll be able to find them easily in the future.

Delete any duplicates until you have the one from each memory you love best. No one needs 10 photos of the exact same thing.

Delete all the screenshots you thought you needed but haven't looked at.

If you want your pics printed, apps like Freeprint and Snapfish are easy to use and you can order straight from your phone.

It's so easy to take pictures nowadays, most of us take far too many and we end up with an overcrowded camera roll. Edit them regularly and it will help to make it less of a laborious job.

A fun and easy way to edit your camera roll is to type today's date (number first, then month) or just the name of the month into the photo search bar and your phone will bring up all the images from that specific date newest to oldest. You will easily find duplicates, screenshots and images you can remove this way.

Seasonal Zone Clean
Week 11: Digital Declutter

4 - PHONE CONTACTS, CALL HISTORY, MESSAGES, NOTES

- Contacts - Go through your contacts on your phone and delete any that no longer need to be there.

- Favourites - Check your favourites list is still relevant Add and delete contacts as required.

- Calls - Check your call list and clear it completely if you don't need it.

- Voicemail - Check voicemails and declutter accordingly. Be careful with this one incase you've saved sentimental messages you want to keep.

- Text messages - Unless you like to keep texts have a check through and see if there are some you can delete. You can 'clear all' in one go if you don't want to keep any of them. It won't be long until they start building up again!

- WhatsApp - WhatsApp is the only item on this list that takes up a LOT of memory space on your phone and is worth editing and streamlining regularly. To check, go to your phone's general settings and click 'phone storage'. You'll instantly see how high up it is on your list. There may be WhatsApp groups you've been added to for an event or a temporary period of time, which you can delete or remove yourself from. You can also set up 'Disappearing Messages' for specific chats to save storage space. Edit and manage your usage and data in your WhatsApp settings.

- Notes - Declutter and tidy up your notes app. Create folders to organise your notes into general categories.

5 - SOCIAL MEDIA

- Unfollow - Check all your social media platforms and unfollow accounts, profiles and groups you've joined that no longer interest you or are no longer relevant. If there are accounts that stress you out or make you feel bad, unfollow immediately. You don't need that in your life. Free up precious time and space for the content you do love that adds to your life in a positive way.

- Declutter and delete - If you create content for social media, it is important to take the time to optimise your bio and profile pages to ensure they are up to date and share the correct information about you or your business. Edit and reorganise your Instagram highlights, delete content you've posted or saved that you no longer want to keep.

- Notifications - If you are being constantly bombarded and distracted by unnecessary social media notifications, it's time to sort it out. Go into your settings in each social media platform and turn off the notifications or adjust the type and frequency. Life will be a little bit more peaceful without them.

- Delete or take a break - If social media is wasting too much of your time or it is affecting you in a negative way, it might be time to say goodbye, at least for a while anyway. Are you active on all your social media accounts? Are there any you don't really use that you wouldn't miss? Delete and detox completely or simply take a break. Try it as an experiment and see how you feel without it.

ZONE 12
Car, Garage, Outdoor Space

Car Delutter
Car clean - interior and exterior
Car and boot reorganise

Garage and garden shed
Declutter, clean & organise

Garden and outdoor space
Sweep paths
Weed paving and borders
Freshen up pots and tubs

Prep outdoor seasonal items

Seasonal Zone Clean
Week 12: Outside

Car/Garage/Outside Space

It's the final week of this season's zone clean and this time we're heading outside!

It's time to give your car a bit of TLC, maybe a quick tidy in the garage or shed, a general spruce up in the garden and a chance to prep and clean seasonal decor, furniture and accessories.

Car Interior
Declutter, Tidy & Vacuum
Grab a bin bag and get rid of any rubbish. We're talking, receipts, food wrappers, water bottles etc.

Declutter all the storage areas: door bins, glove box, boot, seat pockets and centre console bins.

Remove all mats and vacuum along with the upholstery and foot wells. Clean all interior car surfaces with car wipes or warm soapy water and a well wrung out microfibre cloth. Polish the inside of the windows with glass cleaner and a lint free cloth or a damp glass cleaning microfibre cloth.

Car Exterior
Car wash time!
Bucket, car shampoo and sponge at the ready (or microfibre mitt!)
Confession time - I'm not into washing the car. I just don't like doing it, but I do like driving around in a nice clean car, so it is something I prefer to outsource.

However you decide to do it, you'll be glad you did, especially if you did the interior first! For an extra touch, why not treat your shiny, clean and clutter-free car to a new air freshener to make it smell as good as it looks!

Garage / Shed

Spend a wee bit of time giving your garage or shed a quick tidy up.

Hopefully you'll get a nice day. Check the weather forecast and pick the best day this week to do this.

Empty it completely, or just one area of it at a time if it is very cluttered. Clear out the things you no longer use...
Toys the kids have grown out of.
Garden tool duplicates.
Old paint.
Old plant pots.

Sweep the floor, clean the doors and any windows if you have any.

Garden / Outside Space

Give your garden or outdoor space a spruce up.

Sweep, weed and pressure wash patio areas and paths.

Clean garden furniture and outside window ledges.

Weed beds and borders.

Add a few seasonal plants.

Check solar and outdoor lights.

THE HOME RESET

HOME RESET OVERVIEW

Week One Kitchen	**Week Two** Kitchen
Week Three Living Room	**Week Four** Dining Room
Week Five Main Bedroom	**Week Six** Kid's Rooms/ Guest bedroom
Week Seven Bathrooms	**Week Eight** Hall, stairs & entryway

When life gets busy, our homes get busy.

If your house gets a little neglected and out of control from time to time, you're not alone. Things in the wrong place, furniture moved around, piles here and there, a mountain of ironing...you know what I'm talking about.

When this happens, it's time for a Home Reset!

Before I share the tips, let's get clear on what a home reset actually is...

A home reset is the process of getting your home and possessions back to a baseline of clean, tidy and clutter free. A pleasant, functional space where you can live, work, play and relax every single day.

Have you ever tried to clean a room that's cluttered and out of control - only to find yourself going round in circles feeling frustrated and achieving very little? Yep, me too!

This is where the home reset comes in. Think of it like a bootcamp for your home!

A home reset can be done at any time of the year if your home needs it, but resetting in January is the perfect time. What a productive way to get your year off to a great start!

Every person, family and home set-up is unique. Some might manage a different room each day while others will happily manage one room each week. The latter is a bit more manageable and is my personal favourite.

It depends on the space you are working on which tasks you will do. Not everything on the lists will apply.

Your home is your safe space. Your sanctuary from the outside world. Are you ready to make it a place that welcomes you with open arms when you walk through your front door?

Here's how to Reset Your Home in 4 easy steps:

STEP 1: Assess your home

What do you want to change or improve? Which areas are bothering you? How do you want it to look and feel? Take 5 - 10 minutes to walk around your entire home to identify the areas that need attention. Simply take it all in as you visit each space, or jot down notes on a piece of paper to create a list that you can check off. Follow the home reset provided or decide where you will begin based on what you find.

STEP 2: Tidy & Declutter

It's simply not possible to clean a messy house quickly or easily, which is why the next step is to tidy and declutter. Eliminating the excess is fundamental for ease of cleaning and at the same time you will be creating a more serene environment to live in. Try to begin each room's reset with a tidy and declutter session.

You'll need a bin bag, a donation bag (or two!) and a basket or box to collect things that belong elsewhere in the home. Set a timer for 15 - 30 minutes (whatever you can manage) and get to work! When the timer goes off you can stop.

More tips on the next page. $\longrightarrow$

- Work the room in a clockwise direction.
- Tidy the surfaces and floor.
- Pick up and put away, decluttering as you go.
- Let go of things you no longer use, need or love.
- Rearrange furniture if required.
- Plump cushions, fold blankets, make beds.
- Straighten books and magazines.
- Remove dead foliage from houseplants.
- Relocate items to their proper home.
- Do a mini wardrobe edit.
- Declutter the fridge or freezer.
- Pick a cupboard, drawer or shelf to empty, declutter and reorganise.
- Bin the rubbish.
- Bag up anything for donation.
- Remove bags from the home promptly and donate as soon as you can.
- Carry on with your day!

STEP 3: Clean

Now your space is tidy and the excess removed, it should be nice and easy to clean.

Remember, this is a RESET and not a daily or weekly cleaning routine, so it's important not to get caught up with regular everyday chores. Focus on the occasional cleaning jobs that need attention right now. Those tasks we sometimes 'forget' about! See the suggested cleaning list on the next page and pick the ones that make sense to you. Tweak to suit.

You'll need a microfibre cloth or two and warm water. A cloth designed for cleaning glass is also a good idea. Refresh the water and wring out the cloth regularly, replacing it with a clean one when it gets dirty.

Home Reset Cleaning Tasks

- Glass, mirrors and screens, including glass in windows and doors.
- Lighting, light fixtures and lamps.
- Doors and woodwork, including the front door, window ledges and skirting boards.
- Dust the surfaces with a damp cloth.
- Vacuum upholstery and floors, moving furniture where required.
- Shake small rugs outside.
- Kitchen: Clean large appliances - fridge/freezer, oven, dishwasher, washing machine.
- Bathroom: Clean shower.

STEP 4: Style

As you complete the reset of each room in your home, you may wish to style it for the season too. This doesn't have to be complicated. If no big changes are required, keep it simple with a few, simple decor touches here and there.

You could add some greenery to your space with a houseplant or a beautiful vase of flowers. Fresh or faux, you'll get the same stylish result for your home as well as a guaranteed mood boost. Orchids are my absolute favourite. As well as looking very Zen and luxe, they are a more cost effective option than fresh flowers as they last a lot longer and bloom for months!

Another easy addition could be a lovely candle or diffuser in your favourite scent that will subtly fragrance the atmosphere and add a stylish touch to your space.

There you have it, four easy steps to reset your home. Use the ready-made checklist provided in the next chapter, or customise your own reset using the blank template.

THE CHECKLISTS

The daily/weekly checklist examples explained...

It's important to note, I do some of my 'weekly' tasks fortnightly to break it up and make it easier on myself. This means Mondays, Tuesdays and Wednesdays are slightly different each week and why my routine spans 2 checklists. You may not need to do that. It's trial and error to find the best routine for you.

It can look like a LOT when you write it all down but some things are really quick and automatic and only take a few minutes. Look to see where you can delegate jobs to other family members too. You don't need to do it all yourself.

Reminder: for easy bathroom maintenance, I do a quick clean of the toilets and sinks most days followed by **one** other weekly task.

*First a word on showers - always remember to clean your shower when you're in it. Rinse the walls down quickly after your shower and squeegee it or dry it off with a microfibre cloth before you get out. Takes 2 minutes and regular maintenance like this means no big shower scrub required EVER AGAIN! It prevents, or at the very least, reduces mould and mildew forming. If you have a closed shower cubicle, try to leave the door open between showers to allow air to circulate. This task is not on the checklist because it's a habit I do without thinking.

Okay, for the extra weekly bathroom tasks...

Mon - **Mirrors**
Tue - Tub
Wed - **Windows**
Thu - Nothing extra, but let me know if you can think of anything beginning with **Th**!
Fri - Floors

On Mondays and Fridays I change the towels, wipe down the towel radiators and empty the bins. This method means there's no need to clean whole bathrooms at once or have a bathroom cleaning day. With all that said, if you want a bathroom cleaning day, ignore all this and make room for it in your routine.

Experiment with the daily/weekly routine to begin with to see how it goes, then once you get into your groove and find the bits you like, create your own using the blank templates. Having a plan is better than trying to do everything haphazardly.

Above all...
- Please don't feel the need to fill every box.
- If you don't get everything done, don't beat yourself up, it doesn't matter.
- If you missed bits one week, forget about 'catching up', just get back on track the following week.
- Be sensitive to your needs and keep it as simple as you can for your lifestyle.

Daily and Weekly Housekeeping Routine (example)

Month: *January*   **Week:** *1*

DAILY

	M	T	W	T	F	S	S
Make beds	☐	☐	☐	☐	☐	☐	☐
One load of laundry	☐	☐	☐	☐	☐	☐	☐
Plan + prep tonight's dinner	☐	☐	☐	☐	☐	☐	☐
Toilets, sinks + one other	☐	☐	☐	☐	☐	☐	☐
Dishes/dishwasher	☐	☐	☐	☐	☐	☐	☐
Hob + kitchen surfaces	☐	☐	☐	☐	☐	☐	☐
Vacuum/mop if required	☐	☐	☐	☐	☐	☐	☐
Mail/filing	☐	☐	☐	☐	☐	☐	☐
Iron/fold/put away laundry	☐	☐	☐	☐	☐	☐	☐

ZONE OF THE WEEK

Zone 1 - Kitchen

MONDAY

Tidy + clean living rm	☐
Empty bins	☐
Zone clean task	☐
	☐
	☐

TUESDAY

Tidy + clean kitchen	☐
Zone clean task	☐
	☐
	☐
	☐

WEDNESDAY

Change sheets bed 1	☐
Tidy + clean bedroom 1	☐
Zone clean task	☐
	☐
	☐

THURSDAY

Errands/top-up shop/fuel	☐
Tidy handbag/file receipts	☐
Zone clean task	☐
	☐
	☐

FRIDAY

Floors if required	☐
Empty bins	☐
Hall, stairs + landing	☐
Zone clean task	☐
	☐

SATURDAY

Front door + entryway	☐
Water houseplants	☐
Garden/outside space/car	☐
Family/friends time	☐
	☐

SUNDAY

Plan upcoming week	☐
Meal plan/order groceries	☐
Grocery delivery	☐
Ironing if required	☐
Self-care	☐

Daily and Weekly Housekeeping Routine (example)

Month: *January*   Week: 2

DAILY	M	T	W	T	F	S	S
Make beds							
One load of laundry							
Plan + prep tonight's dinner							
Toilets, sinks + one other							
Dishes/dishwasher							
Hob + kitchen surfaces							
Vacuum/mop if required							
Mail/filing							
Iron/fold/put away laundry							

ZONE OF THE WEEK

Zone 2 - Kitchen 2	

MONDAY

Tidy + clean dining rm	
Empty bins	
Zone clean task	

TUESDAY

Tidy + clean utility rm	
Zone clean task	

WEDNESDAY

Change sheets beds 2 + 3	
Tidy + clean bedrooms 2 + 3	
Zone clean task	

THURSDAY

Errands/top-up shop/fuel	
Tidy handbag/file receipts	
Zone clean task	

FRIDAY

Floors if required	
Empty bins	
Hall, stairs + landing	
Zone clean task	

SATURDAY

Front door + entryway	
Water houseplants	
Garden/outside space/car	
Family/friends time	

SUNDAY

Plan upcoming week	
Meal plan/order groceries	
Grocery delivery	
Ironing if required	
Self-care	

My Daily and Weekly Housekeeping Routine

Month: _____   Week: _____

DAILY	M	T	W	T	F	S	S

ZONE OF THE WEEK

_____

MONDAY

TUESDAY

WEDNESDAY

THURSDAY

FRIDAY

SATURDAY

SUNDAY

My Daily and Weekly Housekeeping Routine

Month: _____ Week: _____

DAILY	M	T	W	T	F	S	S
	☐	☐	☐	☐	☐	☐	☐
	☐	☐	☐	☐	☐	☐	☐
	☐	☐	☐	☐	☐	☐	☐
	☐	☐	☐	☐	☐	☐	☐
	☐	☐	☐	☐	☐	☐	☐
	☐	☐	☐	☐	☐	☐	☐
	☐	☐	☐	☐	☐	☐	☐
	☐	☐	☐	☐	☐	☐	☐
	☐	☐	☐	☐	☐	☐	☐

ZONE OF THE WEEK

MONDAY

TUESDAY

WEDNESDAY

THURSDAY

FRIDAY

SATURDAY

SUNDAY

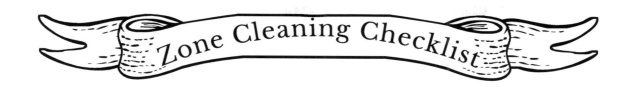

WK 1 KITCHEN

Surface declutter		Cabinet & drawer fronts	
Cabinet/drawer declutter		Counter tops & splashback	
Ceiling, walls & lighting			
Windows/window treatments			
Doors & Woodwork			

WK 2 KITCHEN

Pantry declutter		Dishwasher	
Microwave		Sink Unit	
Oven & hob		Bin	
Fridge		Floor	
Freezer			

WK 3 LIVING ROOM

Surface declutter		Doors & woodwork	
Cabinet/drawer declutter		Fireplace	
Ceiling, walls & lighting		Floor	
Windows/window treatments			
Upholstery/soft furnishings			

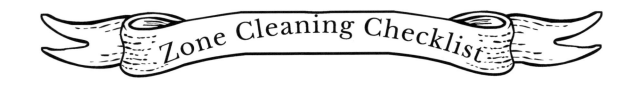

WK 4 DINING ROOM/HOME OFFICE

Surface declutter	☐	Fireplace	☐
Cabinet/drawer declutter	☐	Table & Chairs/Desk	☐
Ceiling, walls & lighting	☐	Floor	☐
Windows/window treatments	☐		☐
Doors & Woodwork	☐		☐

WK 5 WARDROBE EDIT

Hanging clothes	☐	Footwear	☐
Folded clothes	☐	Bags	☐
Lingerie	☐	Accessories	☐
Socks & Hosiery	☐	Jewellery & Watches	☐
Nightwear	☐		☐

WK 6 MAIN BEDROOM

Surface declutter	☐	Doors & woodwork	☐
Cabinet/drawer declutter	☐	Turn mattress/wash protectors	☐
Ceiling, walls & lighting	☐	Floor	☐
Windows/window treatments	☐		☐
Upholstery/soft furnishings	☐		☐

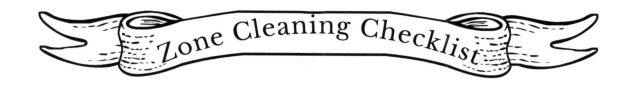

WK 7 KIDS' ROOM/GUEST ROOM

Surface declutter	☐	Doors & woodwork	☐
Wardrobe/drawer declutter	☐	Turn mattress/wash protectors	☐
Ceiling, walls & lighting	☐	Floor	☐
Windows/window treatments	☐		☐
Upholstery/soft furnishings	☐		☐

WK 8 BATHROOM

Surface declutter	☐	Tiles & grout	☐
Cabinet/drawer declutter	☐	Shower	☐
Ceiling, walls & lighting	☐	Taps & plugholes	☐
Windows/window treatments	☐	Sink unit	☐
Doors & woodwork	☐		☐

WK 9 HALL & ENTRYWAY

Surface declutter	☐	Doors & woodwork	☐
Cabinet/drawer declutter	☐	Front door	☐
Ceiling, walls & lighting	☐	Entryway	☐
Windows/window treatments	☐	Floor	☐
Banister	☐		☐

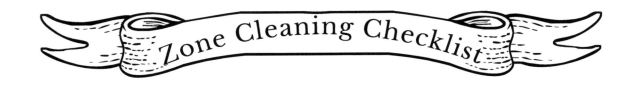

WK 10 UTILITY/LAUNDRY ROOM

Surface declutter	☐	Cupboard & drawer fronts	☐
Cabinet/drawer declutter	☐	Washing machine	☐
Ceiling, walls & lighting	☐	Tumble Dryer	☐
Windows/window treatments	☐	Sink Unit	☐
Doors & Woodwork	☐	Floor	☐

WK 11 ROOM OF YOUR CHOICE/PAPERWORK

Surface declutter	☐	Paperwork declutter	☐
Cabinet/drawer declutter	☐	Mail/magazines/catalogues	☐
Ceiling, walls & lighting	☐	Receipts	☐
Windows/window treatments	☐	Home File	☐
Doors, woodwork & floor	☐	Car/personal/money/home	☐

WK 12 CAR & GARDEN

Car declutter	☐	Garden: tidy borders & pots	☐
Car wash	☐	Garden: pruning & weeding	☐
Car interior clean/vacuum	☐	Sweep paths & clear debris	☐
Garage/shed declutter	☐	Seasonal planting	☐
Garage/shed organise	☐		☐

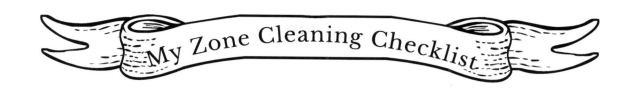
My Zone Cleaning Checklist

WK 1 _ _ _ _ _ _ _ _

WK 2 _ _ _ _ _ _ _ _

WK 3 _ _ _ _ _ _ _ _

My Zone Cleaning Checklist

WK 4 _ _ _ _ _ _ _ _

WK 5 _ _ _ _ _ _ _ _

WK 6 _ _ _ _ _ _ _ _

My Zone Cleaning Checklist

WK 7 _ _ _ _ _ _ _ _

WK 8 _ _ _ _ _ _ _ _

WK 9 _ _ _ _ _ _ _ _

My Zone Cleaning Checklist

WK 10 _ _ _ _ _ _ _ _

WK 11 _ _ _ _ _ _ _ _

WK 12 _ _ _ _ _ _ _ _

Reset Your Home
CHECKLIST

WK 1 KITCHEN

- [ ] Surface declutter
- [ ] Cabinet declutter
- [ ] Drawer declutter
- [ ] Cabinet/drawer fronts
- [ ] Window Interiors
- [ ] Floor
- [ ]

WK 2 KITCHEN

- [ ] Worktop & Splashback
- [ ] Small appliances
- [ ] Oven
- [ ] Hob & Cooker Hood
- [ ] Fridge
- [ ] Freezer
- [ ] Sink Unit

WK 3 LIVING ROOM

- [ ] Surface declutter
- [ ] Cabinet/drawer declutter
- [ ] Windows & Glass
- [ ] Damp dust deep clean
- [ ] Upholstery
- [ ] Floor
- [ ]

WK 4 DINING ROOM

- [ ] Surface declutter
- [ ] Cabinet/drawer declutter
- [ ] Windows & Glass
- [ ] Damp dust deep clean
- [ ] Upholstery
- [ ] Floor
- [ ]

WK 5 MAIN BEDROOM

- [ ] Surface declutter
- [ ] Mini wardrobe edit
- [ ] Drawer declutter
- [ ] Windows & Glass
- [ ] Damp dust deep clean
- [ ] Upholstery
- [ ] Floor

WK 6 KIDS'/GUEST ROOM

- [ ] Surface declutter
- [ ] Mini wardrobe edit
- [ ] Drawer declutter
- [ ] Windows & Glass
- [ ] Damp dust deep clean
- [ ] Upholstery
- [ ] Floor

WK 7 BATHROOM

- [ ] Surface declutter
- [ ] Cabinet/drawer declutter
- [ ] Windows & Glass
- [ ] Shower/tiles/grout
- [ ] Taps & plugholes
- [ ] Floor
- [ ]

WK 8 HALL & ENTRYWAY

- [ ] Surface declutter
- [ ] Cabinet/drawer declutter
- [ ] Windows & Glass
- [ ] Banister & skirting boards
- [ ] Front door
- [ ] Floor
- [ ]

My Home Reset
CHECKLIST

WK 1 _____

☐
☐
☐
☐
☐
☐
☐

WK 2 _____

☐
☐
☐
☐
☐
☐
☐

WK 3 _____

☐
☐
☐
☐
☐
☐
☐

WK4 _____

☐
☐
☐
☐
☐
☐
☐

WK 5 _____

☐
☐
☐
☐
☐
☐
☐

WK 6 _____

☐
☐
☐
☐
☐
☐
☐

WK 7 _____

☐
☐
☐
☐
☐
☐
☐

WK 8 _____

☐
☐
☐
☐
☐
☐
☐

NOTES

Grab a pencil and use this section to get your thoughts down on paper and get clear on what you want for you and your home.

If you want to create your own cleaning routines, remember to consider the 3 layers I mentioned earlier.

1 - Daily Tasks

2 - Weekly Tasks

3 - Zone Cleaning Tasks

I have added some journal prompts to help you on the first few pages and left the rest blank for you to use as you wish.

You may want to draw a rough sketch of your home or the floor plan or simply enjoy making lists.

The blank checklists might come in handy here! Use pencil rather than pen, so you can reuse them as needed.

Have Fun!

Create your vision.
Close your eyes and picture your dream home. What does it look and feel like? Describe it...

What elements from your vision of your dream home could you easily achieve in your current home? Think about the feeling you want to create...

What do you like about your current home? Why?

Is there anything you dislike about your current home? Why?

What would you like to change or improve in your home? Writing down your goals helps to clarify what you want to achieve.
Make a list and arrange into priorities from most important to least important...

How do you feel right now about decluttering, cleaning and keeping your home in order? What's working well? What needs to change? Why?

Your home set up.

How many zones (rooms or areas) do you have? Don't forget your outside space too! Draw a plan or create a list of every area you need to take care of...

Make a list of the tasks required in each zone...

Your existing routine (if you have one).
What do you already do daily, weekly, monthly, occasionally? What works well?

Use the next few pages to outline and create a new routine to try. Remember the checklists are there for you to customise if you wish.

Plan your time...
Where will you find time to declutter, tidy and clean. Think realistically about your current schedule and the time you have available. When do you want to do each task? When are you at your most motivated and energetic? Do you want housework free weekends?

My busiest days/times are...

I feel most energetic...

I would prefer to get tasks done...

The days I want to be free of housework are...

My Daily Tasks and Routine
(Which tasks? When will you do them?)

My Weekly Tasks and Routine
(Which tasks? When will you do them? To make it even easier, are there any tasks you could do fortnightly instead?)

My Zone Clean Tasks and Routine
(What zones? Which tasks? When will you do it?)

NOTES

WHAT TO DO WITH YOUR DECLUTTERED ITEMS

AN A-Z DIRECTORY

Antiques, War Medals and Fine Art:
Local auction houses
Medal specialist
Lladro Collectors Club

Bedding and Towels:
Towels, duvets and pillows - some charity shops and refugee centres as well as animal rescue centres.

Books:
Donating:
Most charity shops
Oxfam have dedicated bookshops across the UK
Selling:
Simply Sell Books accepts all types of books from children's books, hardbacks, school textbooks, ex-library books. They will try and find a home or recycle if not saleable. (It is free to list books).
We Buy Books - quote a price using the ISBN number and organise free postage.

Books, CDs and DVDs:
Ziffit
Music Magpie
School/Academic Books:
Local Facebook groups - offer academic books to students in local area
Book Harvest (England and Wales)

Bras:
Oxfam
Smalls For All
Against Breast Cancer recycling scheme

Bridal:
Stillwhite
Bride2bride

Children's Clothes:
Facebook local selling page/Facebook Marketplace
eBay
Vinted
Jack and Jill Market (Scotland)
mum2mummarket.co.uk - hire a virtual stall, keep 100% of the proceeds
StuffUSell

Cleaning Products:
Food banks
Trussel Trust has branches all around the UK.
Local Women's refuge or refugee centre.
Marigold Gloves - TerraCycle UK website

Clothing & Shoes:
Donating:
High street charity shops
Doorstep Collections
Clothes Aid - will pick up.
British Heart Foundation - will pick up.
Nike - Reuse-a-shoes, drop off at Nike shops
Clarks - drop off at stores
The Air Ambulance - postal donations of good quality clothes, shoes and accessories.
Selling:
We are Thrift
eBay
Vinted
Turtle Doves - recycle cashmere
reThread
StuffUSell

Coffee Pods:
TerraCycle UK
Nespresso
Kerbside recycling in some areas

Exercise and Sports Equipment:
Gymstock 07400 887613
Golf clubs - Golfbidder
StuffUSell will sell things on eBay on your behalf for a fee.

Fabrics:
All charity shops collect textiles in poor condition as 'rags' by weight, so will usually accept all clean textiles whatever the condition. Label your donation bag 'RAGS'

Food:
Food Banks - unopened and within 'Use by' date.
Local refugee centres and homeless charities
Olio - olioapp.com
Trussel Trust

Fur Coats:
Many charity shops will not accept them.
Some theatre groups will accept vintage fur items to use as costumes.
eBay
Vinted
The London Fur Company

Furniture:
The Furniture Re-use Network
British Heart Foundation - free collection within 72 hours
Sue Ryder - free collection within 72 hours

Glasses:
Most opticians have a collection bin
Lions Club will take glasses for recycling

Hearing Aids:
Lions Club
Help The Aged - Hearing Aid Appeal

Linens and Lace:
Local antique dealer

Make Up:
Boots - make-up recycle scheme, collect advantage card points.
Superdrug
John Lewis
Maybelline recycling stations in Superdrug and most large Tesco supermarkets, taking all brands of makeup.

Medical Equipment:
Freecycle or Freegle
Some equipment will have a phone number for the supplier to collect.
Many High Street charity shops accept walkers.
Limbcare for prosthetic limbs, orthotic parts, mobility aids including crutches frames and wheelchairs. They arrange pick up across the UK.
NRS for disability aids and mobility equipment to the NHS. All equipment has a barcode.

Medicines:
Medication must go back to pharmacy/surgery for safe disposal.

Mobile Phones and Computers/Cables and Parts:
Freecycle
Freegle
Most recycling centres accept wires/cables, PCs, mobile phones, laptops etc
*Remember to wipe them first
Green Machine Computers
Variety charity will accept mobiles and cartridges 01372 751 170 for collection.
Hubbub recondition old donated phones. They send a freepost envelope.
Screen-share.co.uk
Computeraid take computers and laptops.

Printer Cartridges:
Tesco Supermarket recycling point

Sanitary Products:
Red Box Project: Have to be in closed box with date visible.
The Trussell Trust - accepts food, household and sanitary items.

Sewing Machines and Tools:
Tools with a Mission
Men's Sheds Association

Sheet Music:
Donations to Oxfam are sorted centrally and sheet music is sold online.
Sheet Music Warehouse - mostly 100 years old or more.

Small Electricals:
Sue Ryder - flatscreen TVs, Hi-Fi systems and small electrical items
Barnados and British Heart Foundation - most take small electrical items. Call to check first.
Local recycling centres and some kerbside recycling
Recycling for Good Causes
Recycle Your Electricals - log on to find your nearest drop off point.
StuffUSell

Socks:
Stand 4 Socks
Shelter
Crisis
Centrepoint
Big Issue Foundation
Depaul UK
Emmaus

Stationery and writing materials:
Ask schools/colleges/universities in your area.
Local Facebook groups
Pens For Kids
Freegle
The Freecycle Network.

Toiletries:
Beauty Bank - unused/unopened toiletries and sanitary products for men, women and children with the exception of perfume/nail varnish/nail varnish remover as these are solvents. Post items at your cost
Gillette razor blades - request a recycling bag online

Toys:
Baby Banks
Loved Before
Toys 4 Life collection points
The Toy Project
The Air Ambulance accept postal donations
Hasbro toys recycle via Terracycle points
LEGO Give Back Box.
Teddy Trust
Mattel playback scheme

White Goods:
British Heart Foundation - accept TVs, fridges, freezers, washing machines and dishwashers in good working order

Wool:
Knit For Peace

Please always make sure your donations are clean, in working order and in a saleable condition.

That's it! You've reached the end of the book.
I hope you found it helpful.

Thank
you

Please get in touch with your feedback.
info@organisewithjen.com

ORGANISE
WITH JEN

Jen is a professional home organiser based in Ayrshire, Scotland where she lives with her husband and two sons.

She works with overwhelmed women and busy families to help them create calmer, happier, more organised homes.

Be it wardrobe, home or lifestyle organisation, preparing for a home move, or a big life event, Jen's simple processes, systems and routines eliminate the excess and create beautifully organised spaces that can be maintained for the long term.

Looking for more tips & advice on how to organise your life? You'll find all that and more on Jen's website and blog:

http://organisewithjen.com

Follow on Instagram & Facebook @organisewithjen and why not join the Facebook group dedicated to helping you achieve more with your Zone Cleaning - Zone Clean With Jen. A growing community of like-minded zone cleaning fans, all with one aim in mind - to run their home like a boss!

Printed in Great Britain
by Amazon

60067824R00107